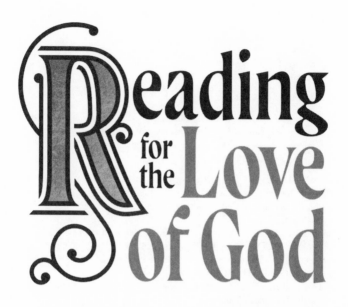

Reading for the Love of God

How to Read as a Spiritual Practice

Jessica Hooten Wilson

Brazos Press

a division of Baker Publishing Group
Grand Rapids, Michigan

© 2023 by Jessica Hooten Wilson

Published by Brazos Press
a division of Baker Publishing Group
www.brazospress.com

Printed in the United States of America

Library of Congress Cataloging-in-Publication Data
Names: Wilson, Jessica Hooten, author.
Title: Reading for the love of God : how to read as a spiritual practice / Jessica Hooten Wilson.
Description: Grand Rapids, Michigan : Brazos Press, a division of Baker Publishing Group, [2023] | Includes bibliographical references.
Identifiers: LCCN 2022037483 | ISBN 9781587435256 (cloth) | ISBN 9781493440535 (ebook) | ISBN 9781493440542 (pdf)
Subjects: LCSH: Spiritual life—Christianity. | Books and reading—Religious aspects—Christianity. | Contemplation.
Classification: LCC BV4501.3 .W55477 2023 | DDC 248.4—dc23/eng/20220912
LC record available at https://lccn.loc.gov/2022037483

The author is represented by WordServe Literary Group, www.wordserveliterary.com.

Baker Publishing Group publications use paper produced from sustainable forestry practices and post-consumer waste whenever possible.

23   24   25   26   27   28   29   7   6   5   4   3   2   1

To Dr. Michael Gose at Pepperdine University,
who taught me the "polyfocal conspectus"
and what it means to "be good."

And to all those who answer the call, "Take, read."

Contents

1

What Kind of Reader Are You?

Imagine you are resting in a cave on an unpopulated Greek island. The other islands in the distance appear nearly as blue as the sky above and the sea below, so that everything before your gaze blends together like an impressionist painting. While staring off into the reverie of blue, a figure of light the size of a skyscraper appears before you, and it seems as though the sun has descended to earth. The being appears as fierce as it is large. A voice rings in your ears: "Go!" It continues commanding you, "Take the little book that is open in the hand of the angel who stands on the sea and on the earth."

Although you did not notice before, this lightning giant holds a small book in its mammoth hands. No one would be brave enough to approach this creature and take anything from it. In fear and trembling, you inch toward the light that the voice has called an angel. You find your voice and croak out the request, "Give me the little book."

Fearing that sentence is surely your last, you do not dare open your eyes. Yet the angel speaks, uttering words even stranger than its form: "Take and eat it."

What do you do? Why and how would you eat a book? The command is followed by a warning: "It will make your stomach bitter, but it will be as sweet as honey in your mouth." The moment reminds you of that time your dad said, "Try this. It's disgusting." But because this is an angel, with much more authority than your father, you do not protest as you did then. Shaking, you nod and take the book. Page by page, tearing the leaves off as if shredding chard, you chew up the book. Unlike an undressed salad, the book melts on your tongue, disintegrating into sugar, as the angel said it would. No sooner do you finish swallowing the final punctuation marks than your stomach begins to turn and writhe. As you fall to the ground, clutching at your stomach, you receive another command: "You must prophesy."

The above is my rewrite of Revelation 10:8–11. The Bible is weird. And lovely. And awe-inspiring. It is like no other book that has ever been written. It is the Book of books, the foundation of every story, and the lens through which Christians see all other books. If we were to read the Bible on its terms, we would become different people, converted by the practice. Christ's vision would become our vision. *Why* and *how* we read matters as much as *what* we read. If we are poor readers, an encounter with the Word will not do much to make us his people. Plenty of people have read the Bible without so much as an eye twitch toward faith. And too many Christians who read the Bible every day forget what love and justice and hope should look like in practice. When a religious teacher tested Jesus on the law, Jesus responded, "*How* do you read it?" (Luke 10:26). It is not enough to read the Bible; you must *eat* the book. You must delight in its honey. Suffer in your gut. And then prophesy. If you want to know how to eat the book, learn how to read— not only the Bible but other great books as well—as a *spiritual practice.* In reading other books, we practice reading the Bible; and in reading the Bible, we read other books by that lens.

Reading Quiz

What kind of reader are you? How do you read now? Let's walk through a quiz, similar to one you might take when trying to figure out your Enneagram or which Hogwarts house in Harry Potter you belong to.

1. What section of the bookstore are you most drawn to (assuming you still enter brick-and-mortar stores and don't just order online)?
   a. Memoir
   b. Self-help
   c. Religion
   d. Literature
   e. Other

2. When picking a book to read for fun, you do so most often by:
   a. Looking at Oprah's Book Club
   b. Listening to friends' recommendations
   c. Finding the book your group is decrying on social media so that you can read it quickly and write a scathing review
   d. Following a great books list like the Harvard Classics or John Senior's "Thousand Good Books"
   e. What's "read for fun"?

3. When thinking about what a book means after you read it, do you mull over:
   a. Your own feelings and thoughts?
   b. The author's intention?
   c. The pages of text?

4. The greatest recommendation a book can receive is that it is:

   a. Thought-provoking and inspiring

   b. Original and new

   c. A page-turner

   d. Relatable and relevant

5. True or False: Books are only the expression of a writer's ideas; they carry no authority or greater significance.

6. With which opinion are you more sympathetic?

   a. "I think we ought to read only the kind of books that wound or stab us. If the book we're reading doesn't wake us up with a blow to the head, what are we reading for?" (Franz Kafka)[1]

   b. I prefer books with instant uplift. I feel good after I read them, as though I can have hope in humanity. Books with a spiritual purpose.[2]

7. Reading is an activity best done:

   a. In silence and solitude

   b. Aurally in community

   c. Depends on the book

8. True or False: If you think a book is good, no one can tell you that you are wrong.

9. With which opinion do you agree?

   a. "A great deal of literature was made to be read lightly, for entertainment. If we do not read it, in a sense, 'for fun,' and with our feet on the fender, we are not using it as it was meant to be used." (C. S. Lewis)[3]

   b. "I cannot live without books, but fewer will suffice where amusement, and not use, is the only future object." (Thomas Jefferson)[4]

10. Consider the following brief descriptions of various types of readers. With which do you most identify?

a. *The no-nonsense literalist:* This reader prefers that the author be a straight shooter. Rather than poetic phrases and metaphors, this reader wants the explanation on the surface. In the words of George Herbert, "How wide is all this long pretence! / There is in love a sweetness readie penn'd: copie out only that, and save expense."[5] When she picks up a book, she has a tendency to skip over the flowery language and get to the main point. If there are lines that don't make sense, this reader mentally crosses them out and moves on. If there are passages that she disagrees with, she'll put the book down and go on to the next book.

b. *The romantic adventurer:* Books are meant for escape. As J. R. R. Tolkien says, "Why should a man be scorned, if, finding himself in prison, he tries to get out and go home?"[6] Escape is a virtue of a good book. This reader most closely identifies with Don Quixote or Catherine Morland from *Northanger Abbey.* If the book is not a page-turner, is it even worth reading? More than ideas or word choices or other small things, what matters is the plot. You want to know what happens.

c. *The liberator:* The world is full of lies, and we need books that tell the truth. Books give us power. We can know more than those who came before us, even if, as T. S. Eliot asserted, "they are that which we know."[7] If we can get the right books into the right hands, people will become better versions of themselves. The "direct pathway from slavery to freedom," in the words of Frederick Douglass, is knowledge.[8] "I conceive that a knowledge of books is the basis on which all other knowledge rests," George Washington said.[9] To that the liberator says, "Amen."

d. *The unfinalizable panoptes:* Because this person is in-process and on a quest, she is never satisfied with her

5

own way of seeing the world. She reads to see how others see the world—the living, the dead, those like her, those different from her, and maybe even how God sees it. In Greek, *pan* means "all" and *optes* means "eyes," so this reader desires all different ways of seeing to be drawn together. Each book, for this reader, is like meeting a new friend, opening another door, finding a new set of lenses. When she walks into a bookstore, she travels to every aisle, collecting epic poetry and new novels and buying books on the periodic table of elements, on the global economy, or on the Peloponnesian War.

There are no right answers to this quiz. Rather than provide an answer key, let me recommend that you continue reading this book. My hope is that these questions provoked you to consider the *ways* you read, and the assumptions you make about how to read, without being fully aware of them. We all bring baggage to our reading, for all of us learned how to read from others. Some of those reading lessons have been quite advantageous, while others may have caused blind spots.

The Profile of an American Reader: Thomas Jefferson

When I was in third grade, I wrote a short biography of Thomas Jefferson. The biography was arranged alphabetically as an acrostic poem, walking through the many roles and jobs that Jefferson had: A for archaeologist, for example, because Jefferson published the first American archaeology report. Jefferson was a man of many talents and many sins, but I am not interested here in digging into controversies regarding his character. What I want to do is examine his reading habits, especially the ways they compelled him to create the Jefferson Bible. If you are not familiar with this piece of Americana, the Jefferson Bible is the nickname given to the "handcrafted, cut-and-paste, compressed version of the Gospels edited by Jefferson with a sharp blade and glue; a book he called *The Life and Morals of Jesus of Nazareth*."[10] He began the project in 1804, excising from the New Testament all but the philosophical claims of Jesus, and he finished it decades later, compelled by his former secretary, who assured him that others would make use of such a book.

As a humanist, Jefferson is an ideal specimen. Jefferson was a product more of the Enlightenment than of the church, more a scientist than a literary figure. In his pockets, he carried around little instruments—thermometers, a compass, a globe. He followed a strict daily routine, never sleeping in late and always filling each hour with an appropriate activity. He set stringent expectations on those around him to create similar to-do lists. When it came to his reading habits, he expected books to be useful to him. Jefferson was not one to waste time in leisure or to delve into a story *merely* for pleasure. Rather than read for delight, Jefferson ensured that he read "something moral" every night before turning in.[11] All reading was submitted to Jefferson's standards of use, relevance, and scientific truth.

For Jefferson, a book must prove its worth, and he was the judge. He applauded Shakespeare, for instance, for his plays' ethical value.[12] Jefferson writes, "Everything is useful which contributes to fix in the principles and practices of virtue. When any original act of charity or of gratitude, for instance, is presented either to our sight or imagination, we are deeply impressed with its beauty and feel a strong desire in ourselves of doing charitable and grateful acts also. On the contrary when we see or read of any atrocious deed, we are disgusted with its deformity, and conceive an abhorrence of vice."[13] One can find such a stance admirable. If we read these sentences apart from any knowledge of the author's life or work, we can agree with much of it. We hope people will cling to what is good and hate what is evil and that they will act graciously rather than viciously after reading great books.

But how does such a morally upstanding person pull apart the Bible and put it back together again according to his own tastes and preferences?

In his biography of the Jefferson Bible, Peter Manseau begins with the tale of Jefferson's archaeological exploits. To prove a hypothesis, Jefferson excavated burial mounds near his land to find out whether such mounds were the site of a battle or the cemetery of the Native Americans. Because Jefferson's contemporaries did not consider Native Americans to be civilized enough to bury their dead in the fashion of Western culture, they conjectured that the discovered bodies may be from a lost race that predated the local Native American tribes. After digging up bodies of infants and children and finding no arrowheads or signs of bullet wounds, Jefferson decided that the mound was the site for Native American burial.

In this story, how do we read Jefferson? Is he a scientist pursuing rightful inquiry and detailing the data, or is he an inconsiderate colonialist desecrating the remains of aboriginal people? Manseau places the episode before readers to have us weigh in our minds "what constitutes that which ought to be inviolable" and how these notions "may alter significantly from one generation to the next, to say nothing of the changes that occur across centuries."[14]

In other words, the practices of reading the Bible during the Enlightenment shaped Jefferson such that he could take a blade to its pages without doubting his faith. "He reordered the passages with little regard for the intention with which they were first composed, repurposing them rather according to his own intuition and sensibilities."[15] Jefferson was well versed in multiple languages, so he compiled his version of the Bible from a 1794 Greek-Latin edition, an 1802 French translation, and an 1804 English translation. According to his biographers, Jefferson started by drafting his own table of contents—a rubric, if you will, for what to include. As a guide, Jefferson drew on the

1778 *A Harmony in Greek of the Gospels* to arrange his verses in chronological order. "Made up of sound-bites of scriptures separated, shuffled, and stitched back together in a way that seeks to supplant rather than serve their original meaning, the Jefferson Bible is less a book than a remix," Manseau observes.[16]

Lord, forgive me if I ever compose a Hooten Wilson Bible. We may find such an endeavor horrifying and arrogant. Yet we should pause and consider whether we have accidentally committed similar errors in the ways we read the Bible. Do we cut and paste verses around our house according to what suits us? On our clothes, our mugs, our cars? I love the sign in my house that quotes Zephaniah 3:17: "The LORD your God is with you, he is mighty to save. He will take great delight in you, he will quiet you with his love, he will rejoice over you with singing." So why is it permissible for our habits of reading to allow us to convert the Bible into consumerist items for purchase but not to become, as Jefferson did to his Bible, a moral guidebook on our nightstand? I am not attempting to justify Jefferson's choices by saying that we may be just as mistaken. I am wondering whether we have inherited Jefferson's ways of reading more than we might realize. I do think we are more American in our way of reading the Bible than we are aligned with church tradition.

As a reader, Jefferson did not limit himself to reading the Bible. He advised one lawyer-in-training to read twelve hours each day, including multiple hours on science and at least a couple of hours in belles lettres before bed. However, Jefferson deemed contemporary novels worthless. In *Books and the Founding Fathers*, George Nash summarizes Jefferson's letter of 1818, in which he wrote a friend denouncing eighteenth-century novels as "a 'mass of trash'—'poison [that] infects the mind' and becomes 'a great obstacle to good education.' Fiction should have moral utility, he argued. 'Nothing of mere amusement,' he declared, 'should lumber a public library.'"[17] I have overheard so many Christians echo Jefferson's distaste for contemporary fiction—unless, of course, it's Christian fiction. However, what Jefferson calls "trash" we now consider classics: *Gulliver's Travels*, *Frankenstein*, *Pride and Prejudice*. A mind that sifts through the narrative of Jesus's life to find the valuable lessons will not easily sit and relish the story of a handmade monster or the drama over the marriages of five sisters.

A Christian Way of Reading

There may be an alternative to Jefferson's way of reading. In contrast to an Enlightenment predisposition, C. S. Lewis was a professor of medieval and renaissance literature. In his book on the subject, Lewis distinguishes between two ways of reading that move readers toward two alternate modes of being. He compares the different methods to two types of travelers. "One man may carry his Englishry abroad with him and bring it home unchanged," Lewis writes. Such a traveler goes abroad, for instance to Italy, and grumbles that the food is not as tasty as that of the local Italian chain back home. He seeks out strangers who share a British accent and visits only the sights where the tourists flock. The visitor decries the *albergo* for not being like a British hotel. Lewis notes, "He complains of the bad tea where he might have had excellent coffee." On the other hand, there is another sort of traveler who exemplifies "another sort of reading": "You can eat the local food and drink the local wines, you can share the foreign life, you can begin to see the foreign country as it looks, not to the tourist but to its inhabitants. You can come home modified, thinking and feeling as you did not think and feel before. So with the old literature."[18] The second traveler has been altered by the country he visited or the book he has read. Rather than fault the foreign country for not being like his home, the second traveler learns to see his home in light of what he learned in the foreign country. He comes home—or he closes the book—with a newly expanded vision.

In 1979 George Steiner labeled these two modes *critic* versus *reader*. To be a critic is to stand over the text, as Jefferson positioned himself above the Bible. "The critical act is a function of the ego in a condition of the will" that makes the critic "*judge* and *master* of the text."[19] This standing *over* prevents the *under*standing necessary to be transfigured by the reading.[20] The reader should approach the book in the way a student draws near a teacher, with a willingness to learn, to receive, from the book. Through the process of standing beneath the text, the reader will be read by the book. And, thus, she will be changed.

Reading in this manner shapes our way of being in the world; it modifies our lenses and vision. While reading cannot induce virtue and cannot make us more Christian by osmosis, the practice of reading well can increase our ways of seeing as contemplatives and beholders, those with imaginations that align more fully with the eyes of Scripture. By practicing certain habits of reading texts, we become those who read even the world with clearer sight.

How to Read as a Christian

On Twitter, someone told me they would never read a book titled *How to Read as a Christian* (the placeholding title of this book). But there is a different way of reading for Christians than for others. For Christ "has subverted the whole order of the old imagination. . . . He illuminates it, and is a new level," as William Lynch professes.[21] We believe in the incarnation, which alters our experience not only of ourselves but of all creation. Everything is spirit and matter. We believe in creation, fall, redemption, restoration. Our God was crucified by his people. Surely all of those beliefs radically affect the way we exist in the world, including how we read. When Jesus asks a religious leader, "How do you read it?" he does not merely want to know *what* the person is reading. The Pharisees and other religious leaders studied the law. They knew the stories of God's faithfulness to his people, from Genesis to Maccabees. Yet, over and over again, especially in the Gospel of Matthew, Jesus feels compelled to ask rhetorically, "Have you not read . . . ?" Apparently, *how* these teachers were reading affected how they lived. It was not enough to possess the right books. Without faithful methods, right motivation, and practices that acknowledge literal and figurative senses of words, these readers were missing the heart of God's revelation.

While much has been written about proper methods of biblical interpretation, I take the question of how to read beyond reading Scripture—what Christians call the "Book of books"—to reading other books. Perhaps it is our digital culture, but we have forgotten our identity as word creatures. God creates the world by word: "Let there be light." And, with a word, God pronounces creation good. He converses with human beings in Genesis through words. He teaches the first human to name the other animals, connecting the stewarding role of human beings with their ability to verbalize. When God enters creation in the incarnation, John describes him as the Word that "became flesh" (John 1:14). From the prophets to the apostles, God reveals himself in words and instructs his people to "write this down" or "eat this book." Human beings are word creatures, and Christians especially should be bookish creatures.

The first time I attended an Anglican church, the most surprising part of the service was when they lifted the physical book of the Bible into the air and carried it down the aisle. People turned and bowed their heads as it moved past them. Their reverence for Scripture captivated my imagination. I had taken for granted that I could hold the Bible in my hands at home, fall asleep reading it in bed. Growing up, some of my friends had Bibles decorated with cartoons. But here, the people of God stood for the procession of the Bible. They stood for the reading of the Word. I felt as though I had been pulled back in time to when

Ezra read the law to the returning Israelites, and they all stood to hear it. Going back to Christianity's Jewish roots, the Torah was carried with worshipers all around it. The people stood for the procession of the sacred word. Jews kissed—and some still kiss—the sacred book when they opened and closed it. If the scroll of the Torah became unusable, they would bury it like a loved one rather than destroy it. The word of God was central to their worship, their culture, their very identity.

From our Jewish mothers and fathers, we Christians inherited this love and reverence for the Word and for words. When Mary the Mother of God accepted the privilege of carrying the Messiah, she responded with words drawn from the Old Testament. She imitated Hannah and Deborah by creating her own hymn of praise, in which she referenced a dozen Scriptures. In the Middle Ages, Mary was depicted in the annunciation paintings with a book before her. It was central to the Christian identity that the mother of the Logos, the woman who carried the Word within her womb, first carried it within her heart. Not only does Mary exemplify a faithful Jew in her attention to Scripture, but she shows Christians what it means to embody the Word.

The early church assumed the necessity of being a bookworm to know God and make him known (though their "books" looked different than they do now). Paul studied Greek myths and knew their ancient stories. He encourages Timothy by reminding him of the inspired nature of the Scriptures and tells him to keep reading and following their story. Many patristic exegetes wrote whole books on how to read, and they invested hundreds of pages in explicating chapters line by line. They defended Homer and Virgil as worthy reading for Christians and imitated their work in their own writings. Although many pagans were illiterate, Jews and Christians were encouraged to know written works, even if they themselves could not read or write.[22] When Rome fell, we could have lost all previous writings to the barbarians. But monks copied and preserved the manuscripts of thousands of poems, myths, and sermons—Christian and non-Christian. Every day, seven times a day, the monks heard the Word of God read, and they chanted along. They knew the Scriptures by memory, and these words were in their minds as they copied beautiful literature, seeing it through the eyes of God's Word.

How We Lost the Art of Reading

So when did Christians stop being considered a bookish people— a people who revered words—those who not only read the Word of God regularly but also read history, literature, philosophy, and the like?[23]

That story is long and complicated, with numerous factors. Some scholars point all the way back to the introduction of spaces between words, when Latin manuscripts moved from organization by syllables to pages of separate words. This change began the gradual descent away from churches filled with well-read Christians. With the conversion from unbroken pages to be chanted in community to separate words on a page, individual reading became possible, leading to less accountability for reading, less shared reading, less connection between the reader and the words on the page.[24] Others consider the printing press and its proliferation of books to have caused the widespread neglect for reading well. Writers needed no authority or expertise or knowledge of the craft of bookmaking to create written works, and thus vicious and ugly works began to be printed among the godly and virtuous ones. How could we know the difference between righteous and unworthy books? Before the advent of mass printing, it had been theoretically possible to read all the great works. After the printing press, how could one read everything? We could even point a finger at the Protestant Reformation and its mistrust of authority, distaste for the scholastics, emphasis on the individual believer, democratization of the Bible, the loss of reading Greek and Latin, and so on.[25]

In the twentieth and twenty-first centuries, we have seen the advent of new forms of technology that compete with books for our attention. Few persons these days could be considered bookish, let alone those in the pews on Sunday. After lengthy days in offices or classrooms or with children, watching Netflix or YouTube is so much easier than reading a book. Over the years in which technology (washing machines, shopping apps, food delivery services) has replaced so many of the arts of life— those domestic responsibilities that used to require craft, such as gardening, cooking, laundry, and so on—we have increased our workloads to replace the energy saved on those other activities. Now we work more and have less space in our lives for leisure. The manual labor of the past that allowed a human being to work in an embodied way, and to contemplate in heart and mind while working with one's hands, encouraged the desire for reading after the physical exertions were completed. One can imagine why a farmer might kick off his boots after a day of sweat and dirt to read a good book. However, I empathize with the struggle that a twenty-first-century accountant, for instance, might feel trying to transition from the headache of the screen to the demands of a literary sentence. Your brain has been frazzled by your work all day while your body has been inactive. If anything, one may assume that zoning out and turning on a podcast or a television show would be easier since those activities require little participation.

Against the seduction of screens, we must return to the love of the book, beginning and ending with the Bible but including other books that enlighten Scripture for us and show us how to live like Jesus in our own time and place. Reading must be a daily spiritual practice for the Christian. A life of reading counteracts the malformation of screen and digital technology. It acts as an antidote to the bad habits of consumerism, utilitarianism, individualism, and other wayward *-isms*. In contrast to many other pastimes, reading demands engagement. It asks something of the participant. It cultivates that person's imagination and increases their vision of the world. While people argue all the time that reading is not a cure-all, no one believes reading is bad. No one doubts that reading—even if it cannot make a person good—can make a person better. But we have to know *how* to read as well as *what* to read.

Following the Reader

In the fourth century, St. Augustine, the bishop of Hippo, wrote a book explaining how to read, aimed at his church congregation. He knew his readers would push back; after all, they had the Holy Spirit. Why did they need to learn how to read? Augustine replies, "Their excitement must be restrained by the recollection that although they have a perfect right to rejoice in their great gift from God, they nevertheless learned even the alphabet with human help."[26] In other words, someone taught you how to read mechanically, so why not learn from another teacher how to read spiritually? Literary theorist Valentine Cunningham steps out further than Augustine: "Reading always comes after theory. We all, as readers, trail behind theory, theory of some kind or another."[27] Even if you never took a college English class, someone taught you to read with certain assumptions about what reading should be like. Whether or not your teacher, your pastor, or your parent was able to articulate their theory of reading, they taught you to read from a specific perspective on reading—what to read, why to read, and *how* to read.

If we are to learn how to read well, I recommend we practice reading according to the ways of those readers we admire. What would it look like to read as Augustine did? Or as Julian of Norwich read? As Frederick Douglass read? As Dorothy L. Sayers? How might we emulate reading with charity, memorizing the best that has been thought and said, and creating from what we read? Throughout this book I'll draw on examples of readers

16

from our past, especially from the church, on how to read the Scriptures, and I'll explore how ways of reading the Bible may be fruitful in how we read literature.

A Teacher in Babel

"The universe (which others call the Library) is composed of an indefinite perhaps infinite number of hexagonal galleries."[28] So begins Jorge Luis Borges's short story "The Library of Babel." In this fictional cosmos, the universe is the library; the library constitutes the whole universe. And the books on the shelves are so infinite that the venture toward knowledge seems meaningless. After all, these repeated books are mere scrambles of combinations of letters in infinite varieties. Each human being is an "imperfect librarian" for the library, which must be "the handiwork of a god." Borges conflates our reading lives and created lives, casting doubt on the meaning of what we read or create. Initially, we may express joy that all answers are available, all sources of knowledge contained before our eyes, if only we can locate the correct shelf. In harmony with this search for meaning, librarians suppose that a key book must exist that deciphers "*all other books*, and some librarian must have examined that book; this librarian is analogous to a god." The superstition of this book and the "Book-Man" parallels the belief in the Bible and the Word that became flesh. While the narrator ends his reflections with an "elegant hope" in a potential order for these books, for the possibility of meaning, those who believe in revelation and the incarnation may end their reading of this story with an even more potent sense of hope. For the books before us may be deciphered; they have a code. We as readers have been granted access to understanding.

In response to this story, Amit Majmudar wrote a sonnet dedicated to Borges. The poem shows us how to stoke the presence of words to life, to participate in the tradition by creating within it. In the opening lines, the narrator stands at a loss before books as numerous as the stars in the sky. You will recognize the image of Borges's library that Majmudar responds to. Then a "blind librarian with a lantern and a hand" takes the narrator's own hand to show the reader where to look. In Borges's story, people await a messianic figure who will decode the contents of the library. Yet, in this poem, only a teacher is needed to direct our attention to one book at a time. As the mentor points his finger, the reader follows, and together they behold with awe as each book, "one by one," opens "into suns."[29]

"READING"
For Jorge Luis Borges

I stand before the books as I might stand
Beneath the night sky. They're in stacks and stacks
of self-contained infinites demanding exploration. I
    have neither maps
nor ladders to pursue these stars,
these books that burn within themselves. That's when
he comes and shows me where to start,
a blind librarian with a lantern and
a hand that takes my own. He knows the books
for me, he knows exactly where they are.
When he points, I at last know where to look.
The deep night sky he navigates by heart,
And as he shows them to me, one by one
I find those far stars opening into suns.

Majmudar might have drawn his "night sky" from C. S. Lewis's metaphor of reading. Lewis writes in *An Experiment in Criticism*, "In reading great literature I become a thousand men and yet remain myself. Like the night sky in the Greek poem, I see with myriad eyes, but it is still I who see."[30] In this image, the act of reading with a guide leads one to contemplation, to an augmented vision. We experience an invitation outside the self through reading, yet the outcome includes a fuller version of the self than one could have created alone. In this sonnet, we are pilgrims. We are Jacob watching the angels ascend and descend. We are readers who long for a guide to take our hand. For Majmudar, the blind librarian is Borges. For Dante, it was Virgil, Beatrice, and St. Bernard. For me, it was initially Flannery O'Connor. My guides have also included Homer, Boethius, Christine de Pizan, Fyodor Dostoevsky, and others. In this book, I hope to point you to those readers who taught me how to read well, so that we too may find books open before us into suns.

2

Why Read Anything but the Bible?

former student wrote me regarding a strange conversation that occurred between her and a friend. Unfortunately, her friend's sixteen-year-old son had begun questioning the faith in which she had raised him. Although the mother tried her best to answer his questions, she had never faced such doubts and was unsure how to respond. My student recommended to her friend that she give her son a copy of *The Brothers Karamazov*. This mother balked: How could a fiction story help my son return to his faith?

As a literature professor, I encounter these doubts fairly regularly. Students sometimes cannot understand the purpose of my literature classes: they confess that they think reading anything except the Bible is unnecessary. However, my former student could not believe her friend had made this retort. She wondered how I would have countered this question. My short answer? Because God revealed himself to us in stories—collected in the Old and New Testaments. Because Jesus told stories to teach about who he is. Because the mysteries of the faith will challenge us our whole lives, and only stories are strong enough not to reduce faith to $x + y = z$. For a longer answer, we should look to the Christian tradition.

"Egyptian Gold" from Augustine's *De Doctrina Christiana*

In *De Doctrina Christiana* (AD 426) Augustine advises readers to learn from human institutions—branches of knowledge—that will aid them in reading Scripture: "This whole area of human institutions which contribute to the necessities of learning should in no way be avoided by the Christian; indeed, within reason, they should be studied and committed to memory."[1] Augustine encourages readers to study not only the mechanical art of reading but also the arts of logic and rhetoric, as well as history, topography, zoology, astronomy, and even the meaning behind numbers and symbols. If we are to read the Bible well, Augustine suggests we try to become amateurs—lovers in the highest sense of that word—of all other human areas of knowledge.

"A person who is a good and a true Christian," Augustine writes, "should realize that truth belongs to his Lord, wherever it is found, gathering and acknowledging it even in pagan literature."[2] His famous allegory on how to glean truth from pagan literature is extracted from the book of Exodus. While Augustine refers specifically to the Platonists in this passage, we can broaden the application of his analogy to include all non-Christian writers:

> Like the treasures of the ancient Egyptians, who possessed not only idols and heavy burdens, which the people of Israel hated and shunned but also vessels and ornaments of silver and gold, and clothes, which on leaving Egypt the people of Israel, in order to make better use of them, surreptitiously claimed for themselves (they did this not on their own authority but at God's

command, and the Egyptians in their ignorance actually gave them the things of which they had made poor use) [Exod. 3:21–2; 12:35–6]—similarly all the branches of pagan learning contain not only false superstitious fantasies and burdensome studies that involve unnecessary effort, which each one of us must loathe and avoid as under Christ's guidance we abandon the company of pagans, but also studies for liberated minds which are more appropriate to the service of the truth, and some very useful moral instruction, as well as the various truths about monotheism to be found in their writers.[3]

Augustine compares reading pagan writers to the Israelites carrying gold out of Egypt. Although the Egyptians employed the gold to fashion idols, God did not deem the gold itself impure but commanded the Israelites to cart it out of Egypt and subject it to their own uses. In the same manner that the Israelites discovered goods—namely, gold—among the Egyptians, Augustine claims that we may find truths within pagan literature. We must sift through the superstitions to claim the moral goods.

Traveling Supplies for Eternity

A contemporary of Augustine, Basil the Great, suffered under a similar protest from his fourth-century monks that we twenty-first-century teachers endure: students who cannot understand why we would waste our time reading anything outside the Bible. Apparently, this is not a new problem. In an address to these young readers, Basil begins by agreeing with his students that the Bible is the most important text to read, for we are destined for eternal life: "Whatever, therefore, contributes to that life, we say must be loved and pursued with all our strength; but what does not conduce to that must be passed over as of no account."[4] The Bible acts as the standard by which all other reading is measured. As immortal creatures, we should judge books outside of the Bible by whether they foster sanctification and increase our knowledge of holy things.

However, we also must admit that the Holy Scriptures are difficult to understand. Perhaps, then, we consider outside reading as preparatory for reading the Bible. With *Goodnight Moon* and Shel Silverstein, for example, we learn how to read mechanically. Then, with Phillis Wheatley and *Jane Eyre*, for instance, we learn how to read poetic tropes, figures of speech, narrative strategies. We practice how to read well and increase our ability to read so that we can know the Scriptures better. Basil compares our task to that of dyers who "first prepare by certain treatments whatever material is to receive the dye, and then apply the color. . . . So we also in the same manner must first, if the glory of the good is to abide with us indelible for all time, be instructed by these outside means, and then we shall understand sacred and mystical teachings."[5] We begin the journey to reading the Bible well by first learning how to read and how to think at all. Then we learn history, science, rhetoric, languages, and so on. These liberal arts provide additional tools by which we can decipher meaning in the Scriptures. After this kind of liberal education, we may, "like those who have become accustomed to seeing the reflection of the sun in water," Basil suggests, "direct our eyes to the light itself."[6] Like lifting lighter weights before the heaviest ones or like climbing the less steep section of the mountain before attaining the summit, reading human literature prepares us to encounter the divine Scriptures.

Once we are able to delight in the mystery of the Word, we do not forgo other literature, but we look within nonsacred books for what Basil calls "travel-supplies" for eternity. As bees who flit from flower to flower to possess the honey while ignoring the thorns, Basil writes, so readers should be drawn to the passages in which writers "have praised virtue or condemned vice."[7] Basil names Homer and Plato as examples of those writers of eternal goods. From Basil's perspective, Homer uplifts heroes for being heroic, and Plato rightly castigates the sophists. Thus, we can glean from these truth-sayers goods for our eternal journey. With a spirit of inquiry, we should follow Basil's example and ask, What in this book praises virtue as the Bible defines virtue? In a similar spirit to Scripture, what condemns vice? Since the time of Basil, there have been many writers who have shown us what it means to live a good life in accordance with the Word of God. For me, I have learned about forgiveness from *The Brothers Karamazov*. I have learned about freedom of conscience from Aleksandr Solzhenitsyn, about dying well from Ernest Gaines, about loving what is beautiful from Sigrid Undset. For the adventure of eternity, Basil exhorts us "to acquire travel-supplies, leaving no stone unturned, as the proverb has it, wherever any benefit towards that end is likely to accrue to you."[8] Or, as St. Paul writes in Philippians 4:8, whatever is true, noble, admirable, think on these things.

To Delight and to Instruct

We have forgotten the purpose of reading when we ask the question, What good is anything outside of the Bible? Since 19 BC, when Horace penned *Ars Poetica*, it has been axiomatic that good literature should accomplish two things: delight and instruction. Horace writes, "Poets wish to benefit or to please, or to speak / what is both enjoyable and helpful to living. . . . Who can blend usefulness and sweetness wins every / vote, at once delighting and teaching the reader."[9] Enjoyable and helpful, useful and sweet, delighting and teaching should be our simple guide for what to read outside of Scripture.

In the sixteenth century, Philip Melanchthon and others riffed on this classical mantra, defending the reading of great literature to their Reformation chums. Melanchthon calls these works the "admirable gifts of God" and uplifts them to second place beneath Scripture—"Apart from the Gospel of Christ this world holds nothing more splendid nor more divine."[10] For Melanchthon, we become slaves to our lower natures when we ignore these riches that bring enjoyment and edify us. The classics refine us toward our higher nature, showing us that we are made in God's image. Melanchthon credits Homer in particular with being "roused by divine power [and] inspired by divine virtue."[11] While not suggesting that the *Iliad* and the *Odyssey* carry any spiritual authority, Melanchthon treats the works of great literature like they are teachers who move us from milk to meat in our spiritual growth.

However, even literature that does not necessarily teach us spiritual truths can be loved for its beauty. Beautiful things still draw from that eternal fount, which is God. In *The Love of Learning and the Desire for God*, Jean Leclercq describes how the medieval tradition read literature and why they invested so much time into copying manuscripts. In short, they read and copied because they loved what was worth loving. "If they read and copied Ovid, for example," Leclercq writes, "it is because his poetry is admirable. At times they drew moral lessons from these authors, but they were not, thanks be to God, reduced to looking to them for that. Their desire was for the joys of the spirit and they neglected none that these authors had to offer. So, if they transcribed classical texts it is simply because they loved them."[12] They found the stories of Ovid and Homer beautiful, despite the pagan gods and secular morality. Whatever is worth loving, we should practice loving.

What Good Is Reading Literature for the Christian?

C. S. Lewis compares the question, "What is the good of reading what anyone writes?" to the question, "What is the good of listening to what anyone says?"[13] No one would ask preachers to stop explicating Scripture on Sunday because nothing should be added to the gospel. Churches often hold book clubs or Sunday school classes on the latest Christian-living book without wondering whether we should read books other than the Bible. Only when the books are poetry, biography, fiction, or some other humanities genre do we balk at the necessity of such reading. How could it be beneficial to the life of a believer to read the belles lettres, the classics, the great books?

"Unless you contain in yourself sources that supply all the information, entertainment, advice, rebuke and merriment you want, the answer is obvious," Lewis responds. We are not self-contained entities with the ability to unpack Scripture and all its mysteries. Rather, we should look to other books the way we seek spiritual teachers, models, and leaders in our faith to guide us. Lewis adds, "And if it is worthwhile listening or reading at all, it is often worth doing so attentively."[14] If we are going to read—the Bible included—we should learn how to read well. We should become readers who do not read for our own gain but who read as a spiritual practice, always open to how the Lord is planting seeds in our heart, teaching us more about him, and showing us ways of living more like Christ in the world.

The Difference between the Bible and Other Literature

Recognizing the Bible as literature opens us up to a fuller appreciation of the holy book than if we treat it like an instruction manual or to-do list. The Bible is a bibliography of genres, including poetry, song, lament, prophecy, history, narrative, parables, letters, dreams, and so forth. We should practice reading in such a way as to enjoy the fullness of that literary experience. However, being divinely authored by God, the Bible also stands apart from all literature penned by human authors. God inspired human writers to pen the words that we receive, but God also authorized those pages. No matter what other beauty, truth, and goodness may be found elsewhere, other works of literature lack the same authority over Christians as the work of Scripture has.

We may read with a certain freedom when it comes to Scripture, which is not the case with nonsacred writings. In Paul's second letter to Timothy, he assures the young disciple, "All Scripture is God-breathed and is useful for teaching, rebuking, correcting and training in righteousness, so that the servant of God may be thoroughly equipped for every good work" (2 Tim. 3:16–17). Our Judeo-Christian Scriptures provide an assurance of their authority—literally, their author is God—as well as their usefulness for forming readers into righteous servants and for gifting us with the power for kingdom work. This authority of the Scriptures relieves readers of the burden to sift through what is fallible and what is divine.

Over years of reading, we may begin to trust certain authors and regard them as teachers, but there remains a difference between their genius and the authority of the apostles. I trust Fyodor Dostoevsky, Eugene Peterson, Fleming Rutledge. By God's grace, any person, any book or artwork, any element of God's creation may speak to a heart. But no matter how much truth or beauty these writers engender, they do not possess the apostolic authority granted to the writers of Scripture. In 1847 Søren Kierkegaard outlined the difference between an apostle and a genius: "Genius is what it is of itself, i.e., through that which it is in itself; an Apostle is what he is by his divine authority."[15] Confronting the manifold theological arguments that focused on Paul's rhetorical or aesthetic brilliance as a writer, Kierkegaard reminds readers that Paul's Letters belong to a different category of assessment. "When someone with authority says to a person, go! and when someone who has not the authority says, go! the expression (go!) and its content are identical; aesthetically it is, if you like, equally well said, but the authority makes the difference."[16] Whether or not you the reader approve of an apostle's style matters less in view of eternity than whether you heed the message and submit your life to its authority.

Other literature may act as a gloss on divine Scripture, responding to the authoritative book with exposition, praise, poetry, narrative creations, and so forth, but none of them carry the weight of the inspired Word. When reading works by geniuses, to use Kierkegaard's label, the readers must evaluate those works as true, good, or beautiful. Unlike the fealty we show to Paul, we owe no obedience to Rembrandt, Gabriel García Márquez, Tchaikovsky. In a metaphor in which Kierkegaard compares a genius to a bird, he writes, "It is modest of the nightingale not to require any one to listen to it; but it is also proud of the nightingale not to care whether any one listens to it or not."[17] Like the nightingale, the genius has an "immanent telos," Kierkegaard says, meaning that the end of the work lies within this plane of existence. The genius's book or art may or may not extend through time, being praised for generations, but ultimately that work is not eternally mandated. There may be glimpses of eternity highlighted by a genius in their art, but such reflections of divine reality are not sanctioned in the genius. Instead of the obedience owed to the apostles, geniuses only request our attention.

BOOKMARK 1

———•———

Reading like Augustine of Hippo

G. K. Chesterton once retorted, in opposition to Oscar Wilde's claim that sunsets could not be valued, by insisting, "Oscar Wilde was wrong; we can pay for sunsets. We can pay for them by not being Oscar Wilde."[1] He meant that gratitude could be expressed through a life well lived. In parallel, we could exhibit our appreciation for the gift of books by reading them with charity. Augustine provides a counter to secular ways of reading, whether sacred or nonsacred texts. For books not authored by God, how might we apply these lessons of being humble, hospitable, and charitable readers? Instead of wristbands that remind us "What Would Jesus Do?" let's make a bookmark: "How Would Augustine Read?"

Augustine the Reader

"As with many immensely fertile thinkers, it is difficult to imagine Augustine as a reader," so says Augustine's biographer Peter Brown. But, of course, as Brown well knows, it is impossible for such a fruitful thinker not to have been sown with seeds from many other writers before him. Brown emphasizes Augustine's debt to the philosopher Plotinus, whose work Augustine "thoroughly absorbed" and "digested."[2] In his *Confessions*, Augustine borrows from Plotinus and also mentions Cicero, Plato, Ambrose, Terence, and Virgil. While many readers have walked away from *Confessions* convinced that Augustine denounces pagan literature, his conversion narrative alludes to and even imitates parts of the *Aeneid*. For instance, notice how Augustine lies to his mother Monica, as Aeneas deceived Dido, to leave Carthage for Italy. Or how Augustine stands with Monica on the shores of Italy before she crosses into death, a moment that alludes to Aeneas's final conversation with Anchises.

What sticks with readers of *Confessions* is Augustine's lament that he ever read the *Aeneid* because of the tears he shed for Dido. But we have to put these statements into context. First, in *Confessions*, Augustine derides his unconverted self for treating these stories solely for their temporary enjoyment. Augustine scholar Brian Stock divides these ways of reading in Augustine's work as aesthetic versus ascetic: "The aesthetic can be defined as a type of reader's response in which the pleasure of the text is an end in itself, while the ascetic assumes that the text is a means for attaining a higher, more pleasurable end."[3] In other words, Augustine worries when we love the Egyptian gold for itself rather than surrendering the gold to God's purposes, as the Israelites did by eventually building God's altars. As a pagan, Augustine wept more for Dido than for the sins of his soul, and therein lies the problem—not in the *Aeneid* but in the wayward reader.[4]

Moreover, Augustine distinguishes between stories that lead one away from truth and those that lead one toward it. Stock notes that Augustine defines mimetic arts, such as painting, sculpture, and other letters and languages, as human-made sign-givers that seek "similitude through signifying."[5] For instance, imagine the way that *The Lord of the Rings* tells the truth about the world through fantasy. While elves and wizards are not empirically real, the story truthfully shows how we can only control the means of action and not the ends, that the lowest among us should be lifted up, that we must all play a role in the Theo-drama, and so on. All of these truths are signified in the story *The Lord of the Rings*. The author is creating mimetic art.

In contrast to this truth-telling in fiction, there are novels that lie to people, whether or not the author intends to, because they do not imitate the world as it is. These writers distort natural law or succumb to deceptions about the world. For example, a story may show you that all your dreams will come true if you wish hard enough, or that even bad people deserve good things, or that rebellious teenagers can gain a happily ever after by disobeying their parents and forging their own way. For Augustine, as a young boy without knowledge of how to read spiritually, the story of Dido and Aeneas did not lead him toward truth. Only after Augustine becomes a Christian does he understand how to read the *Aeneid* figuratively as that which can tell the truth about the world.

When Augustine alludes to the *Aeneid* in *Confessions*, he is modeling how to read the poem, teaching his Christian readers how to interpret and engage pagan literature. He confesses to his emotions being swayed by the *Aeneid*, but then he redirects his weeping toward its rightful end—toward being penitent before God. If the poem is cathartic without the spiritual redirection, then Augustine would ask, what is its purpose? Augustine incorporates and draws from what is good in Virgil's poetry. As one Augustine scholar points out, "This juxtaposition of Vergilian and Biblical figures is a critique of the pagan text, but not merely that. It is also a reinterpretation. Read aright, the desires and griefs of Vergil's character point to the same longings and values as Scripture, and the Scriptural figures illuminate the real significance of the Vergilian for us."[6] By reading Virgil's narrative spiritually, Augustine shows his readers better ways of understanding the true story of the Bible and the stories of their own lives.

Augustine Learns to Read

Augustine comes to learn spiritual reading from St. Ambrose, who oversaw his baptism in Milan. Originally, Augustine thought he would convert to placate his mother and to arrange a prodigious marriage to a Christian woman. However, Ambrose's mentorship, life, and preaching eventually led Augustine to the faith. In *Confessions* Augustine recalls Ambrose's strange reading practice of reading silently, a practice that inspires Augustine to wonder about the reality of the man's faith:

> When [Ambrose] was reading, his eyes ran over the page and his heart perceived the sense, but his voice and tongue were silent. . . . We saw him silently reading and never otherwise. . . . We wondered if he read silently perhaps to protect himself in case he had a hearer interested and intent on the matter, to whom he might have to expound the text being read if it contained difficulties, or who might wish to debate some difficult questions.[7]

Until approximately the twelfth century in the West, vocalized reading was the norm. Reading was a communal practice in which others could hear what was being read. If Ambrose read silently, he was reading only for the transformation of the inward man. He personally consumed and digested the text, a process unshared by external observers, a sight new to Augustine. *Confessions* evidences how the life of the inward self becomes significant for Augustine.

Ambrose taught Augustine how to read not only silently but also spiritually. Prior to Ambrose's instruction, Augustine had considered the Bible foolish because he read it literally. The Manichaeans ask the young Augustine indicting questions such as, "Is God confined within a corporeal form? has he hair and nails?"[8] Uninitiated into spiritual reading, these questions stir in Augustine contempt toward the seeming silliness of Scripture. What kind of God has hair and nails? He confesses, "I had not realized God is a Spirit (John 4:24), not a figure whose limbs have length and breadth and who has a mass."[9] Ambrose teaches Augustine that God, as a spirit, intends his words to be interpreted literally and spiritually, the latter as the higher meaning of the text. Listening to Ambrose preach, Augustine hears "first one, then another, then many difficult passages in the Old Testament scriptures figuratively interpreted," whereas he had, "by taking them literally, found them to kill (2 Cor. 3:6)."[10] This spiritual method of reading opened Augustine to the faith.

Preceding Augustine by a century, Origen of Alexandria wrote commentaries on the books of the Bible that show how to read spiritually. In his exposition of the Song of Solomon, Origen explains the relationship between literal and figurative reading of Scripture: "It is possible for us to mount up from things below to things above and to perceive and understand from the things we see on earth the things that belong to heaven."[11] We seek the spiritual meaning through the particularity of the literal. Augustine did not discard the literal meaning of the text for the spiritual. He attempted a literal interpretation of Genesis but only made it to chapter 3—that's how much attention he pays to the literal. In defense of his way of reading, Augustine explains, "All divine scripture is twofold. . . . In all the holy books, however, one ought to note what eternal realities are there suggested, what deeds are recounted, what future events foretold, what actions commanded or advised. So then, in accounts of things done, what one asks is whether they are all to be taken as only having a figurative meaning, or whether they are also to be asserted and defended as a faithful account of what actually happened."[12] Inherited from Ambrose, this twofold method for reading Scripture governed faithful interpretation for several centuries.

Wary of spiritualizing the text, the sixteenth-century Reformers cautioned readers to return to literal interpretations. They wanted to ensure that readers upheld the authority of Scripture and did not doubt its truthfulness. However, Augustine and the early church writers did not consider spiritual interpretation to undermine the historical and literal truthfulness of Scripture. What is figuratively true is spiritually true, in their readings; in fact, what is spiritually true is deeper and more eternally true than what can be literally validated. If a literal way of reading Scripture would cause the meaning to be unaligned with God's charitable character, then Augustine advises turning to figurative interpretation. In *De Doctrina Christiana*, Augustine clarifies the proper use for spiritual reading: "One should proceed to explore and analyze the obscure passages, by taking examples from the more obvious parts to illuminate obscure expressions and by using evidence of indisputable passages to remove the uncertainty of ambiguous ones."[13] In other words, draw on the clear portions of the text to understand the mysterious ones. Avail yourself of a spiritual reading when a literal reading would not make sense. In this way, the spiritual reading takes priority over the literal, while never abandoning the literal.

The Bible Reads the World

When students first read *Confessions*, they are distracted at the outset by all the references to Scripture. Augustine seems never to write a sentence without quoting, citing, or alluding to the Word of God. Here is an autobiography that shows forth a life under the gaze of God; hence it is also called a "spiritual" autobiography. Whenever Augustine relates an episode from his own story, he seems to be asking, How does God see this scene? Why did God write this part of my life in this way? What could readers learn about God from this time in my life? For Augustine, the Bible becomes the lens by which he reads all other books, history and contemporary events, even his own life. "Reading his Bible, Augustine had come to see the events around him as part of an ineluctable process," Brown notes, "foretold a thousand years before, by David in the Psalms, and by the prophets of Israel."[14] History begins with God creating the world. God is the author of the whole story, of each individual story, and of the stories found in revelation. That's why Augustine returned to Hippo with the desire to found a monastery and be immersed in the Word. If we are to read as Augustine does, we should be seeking out God's intention and meaning as the truth in the texts before us. If the book we are reading does not point toward a spiritual reality, we should recognize its lack. Even that wanting is another testament to spiritual truth.

Reading the Bible as Augustine Does

Augustine assumes that even if one begins to read the Bible without the prerequisite humility, the Bible will humble the reader. For "many and varied obscurities and ambiguities deceive those who read casually, understanding one thing instead of another; indeed, in certain places they do not find anything to interpret erroneously, so obscurely are certain sayings covered with a most dense mist. I do not doubt that this situation was provided by God to conquer pride."[15] How many of us have experienced what Augustine describes? The Bible was not written in our time and place, all at one time, or by one human author. So much of it creates hurdles for our imaginations to jump. Consider the title of a 2020 book: *How (Not) to Read the Bible: Making Sense of the Anti-women, Anti-science, Pro-violence, Pro-slavery and Other Crazy-Sounding Parts of Scripture.* As Augustine said and this title echoes, parts of Scripture sound insane, or at least incomprehensible, because we are human readers, and God is a divine author. Interpretation, then, is a humbling exercise.

If God is far above us, his book must also be beyond our immediate reach. "A God you understood would be less than yourself," Flannery O'Connor writes.[16] Yet, because God is unassuming, he condescends to reveal himself to us, and through his Spirit, he enables us to reach him. Anyone who is haughty may walk away from the text, but the humble seeker will be rewarded by a continual turn to the Scriptures. Augustine notes, "Thus the Holy Spirit has magnificently and wholesomely modulated the Holy Scriptures so that the more open places present themselves to hunger and the more obscure places may deter a disdainful attitude."[17] When a passage does not communicate truth or goodness explicitly, our hunger for God and knowledge of him increases.

Although God reveals himself to us in his Word, interpretation requires effort and dedication. As we work to know God, we increase in humility and love for him. "What is sought with difficulty is discovered with more pleasure," Augustine observes.[18] Consider an analogy between eating and reading. While cotton candy is sweet and does not even require teeth to eat it, it will not fill up one's stomach. On the other hand, steak requires us to sink our teeth in and chew. We work at it, cutting it into smaller chunks, eating slowly, digesting, and enjoying its fullness for a greater amount of time. So, too, with good reading, such as the Word of God. Mary Carruthers points out how common this metaphor was for the medieval imagination: "The more [texts] need 'chewing,' the more difficult they are, the richer their nourishment for a mind engaged in memory work."[19] The work that interpretation requires is paid back a hundredfold in delight and edification.

What then does a humble interpreter look like? Augustine exemplifies the meek reader by asking questions of the text and hesitating to assert his claims when he is uncertain. Observing how Augustine reads Genesis in his work *The Literal Meaning of Genesis*, Hans Boersma notes not only how Augustine confronts the text "with a host of questions" but also how he "openly admits that the meaning is not quite clear to him, and he fails to make a choice among the various options that he has presented."[20] Augustine does not want to master the text or to show readers his correct interpretation of Scripture. He assumes many readers will arrive at a multiplicity of interpretations: "What difficulty is it for me, I say, if I understand the text in a way different from someone else, who understands the scriptural author in another sense? In Bible study all of us are trying to find and grasp the meaning of the author we are reading."[21] Perhaps unlike some contemporary biblical scholars who seek for one right way to interpret the Bible, Augustine allows for more meanings than one person could devise. His goals as a reader are unpretentious: through the words given, Augustine longs to understand the author. He reads the Bible from a humble desire to know God.

We will see that the early church writers as a whole did not view the Scriptures instrumentally or referentially; they considered reading an encounter with the divine. When you recall all the ways that people were transformed or transfigured in the Bible following their experiences with God, you'll have a mosaic of images of what may happen when we find God there. We could be maimed like Jacob, glow radiant like Moses, fall on our knees in tears like Mary Magdalene. Augustine summarizes our response to this meeting, what we call reading: "So anyone who thinks that he has understood the divine scriptures, or any part of them, but cannot by his understanding build up this double love of God and our neighbor, has not yet succeeded in understanding them."[22] What begins in humility for the reader should be transfigured into an increase in charity—both vertically toward God and horizontally outward to our neighbors.

The Requisite Silence

We can imitate Augustine's silent reading, his spiritual approach, his humble motivation, and his dedication to increase in charity.

Our twenty-first-century habits predispose us to silent reading rather than communal; both have a place in the reading life, but let's contemplate the benefits of the former. Ambrose read silently for sustained meditation on the words. By adopting this practice, Augustine cultivated an inner life that birthed his spiritual autobiography, *Confessions*. Only after writing this reflective narrative was the bishop able to finish writing his *De Doctrina Christiana*.[23] Looking inside himself was a necessary precursor to completing the didactic book he had been writing. Likewise, the opening section of John Calvin's *Institutes of the Christian Religion* encourages sinners to begin their journey toward God with a knowledge of the self: "Every person, therefore, on coming to the knowledge of himself, is not only urged to seek God, but is also led as by the hand to find him."[24] Calvin implores us to consider ourselves so we might comprehend all that we lack and thus hope for a God who is perfect to overcome our faulty nature with his abundant grace. One cannot be a teacher without first spending time as a silent student.

While we need such practices of silent reading and meditation, our current culture distracts us from this practice. We are losing our patience for sustained, silent reading. In a 1996 essay, "Letter to Jorge Luis Borges," written a decade after Borges's passing, Susan Sontag laments that "books are now considered an endangered species. By books, I also mean the conditions of reading that make possible literature and its soul effects." She writes of her worries years prior to the invention of smartphones. Yet, seeing the advent of the e-reader, Sontag prophesies that this forthcoming technology will threaten what reading should be. She is thinking about how the new technology provides interaction with the text via the screen, allowing one to highlight and annotate and search definitions. For Sontag, when one can interact with the text, the book is further objectified and limited to its utility. These developments mean, in her words, "nothing less than the death of inwardness—and of the book."[25] We should protect space in our days for silent reading with the same fervency with which we should clear out our schedules for prayer and devotion. Time spent reading might be fertile ground by which the Lord shows us who we are. With that time, the Lord can weed out the lies of culture, convict us of our fallenness, and reveal to us our higher destiny in him. Whereas we may be deformed by hours of screens, we can be recast in his image by the practice of silent reading.

Twofold Method: Spiritual Reading

"Please help me to get down under things and find where You are," Flannery O'Connor prayed during her time at Iowa State University, where she was pursuing a master of fine arts degree in creative writing.[26] She was learning, as a writer, how to dig beneath the surface—the literal—to discover God at work—the spiritual. Augustine teaches us this twofold method of reading (we will investigate the three senses of the spiritual later) that can apply well to reading literature. Through fantastic stories, literature reveals spiritual reality, that we may imagine our world as enchanted with this second layer of meaning. We've all read books that we thought would not translate well into films or even plays because so much of the action of the book occurs within the spiritual undercurrent. To lay bare the dramatic action without being able to demonstrate the spiritual transformation would be to lose the story.

Other stories may become thrilling films, but we digest their spiritual meaning without reasoning through it. A well-known example is the Harry Potter series—such a wild ride of a story with characters of complex personality and dynamic development over the course of several years. The story becomes a fable about sin, how darkness implants itself within you and can gain strength if you allow it, or you can choose self-sacrifice, friendship, and generosity as your combatants against that power.

The story tells the truth about how death to self overcomes fear of death, about how power corrupts from within until you're enslaved to it, and how good people who do nothing become complicit when evil gains strength. We can interpret these books on a spiritual level for what they show us about the things we know to be good and evil from scriptural revelation.

However, when the Harry Potter novels were initially released—and perhaps even now—evangelical parents decried the books for containing sorcery, witches, and use of magic. These same parents may have permitted their children to read the Chronicles of Narnia, books predicated on "deep magic," also with witches and dragons (granted, they're shown as evil), magical potions, and so forth. We cannot judge books on surface-level depictions. Witches and dragons must not always be read as symbols of evil and thereby systematically, thoughtlessly denounced. Does the witch act ethically in the world? Does the dragon portray greed as evil and kindness as a good? Looking past the surface level of symbols, how is magic treated? As mysterious? Capable of destructive power, if used wrongly? A gift? Reading spiritually also means reading beyond the simplistic. That does not mean we endorse all witch stories or stories of vampires or werewolves or whatever mystical creations can be devised. But spiritual reading will teach you how to discern what is good and true about a book, not merely what is off-putting or wears the veneer of depravity.

The Bible Tells Me So

If we read the Bible as our foundational book, we should embody it as we live our lives, becoming God's body in the world, becoming like the Word in the world. Augustine so thoroughly imbibed the Word of God that he could not help but quote it when he read episodes of his life and recorded them in *Confessions*. As readers, we should be underlining sections of books and identifying the truths that accord with what we know of God. In *The Brothers Karamazov*, how does Father Zosima's distinction between love in dreams and love in action gloss 1 Corinthians 13 for us? Reading *A Gathering of Old Men*, we may understand Isaiah's refrain for justice more fully as it applies to our own time. Or, in Shūsaku Endō's *Silence*, the living martyrdom of Father Rodrigues versus those who died for the faith complicates our understanding of taking up our crosses (Matt. 16:24–26). Our reading of other literature should be in constant dialogue with our Bible reading.

Under the condition of biblical embodiment, we can read everything else and find where the image of Jesus Christ is reflected. "Christ plays in ten thousand places," and it is our joy to find where he is and disclose his presence to the world.[27] When I was in college at a Christian university, we sometimes sought the Christ figure in literature: Uncle Tom in *Uncle Tom's Cabin* or Sydney Carton in *A Tale of Two Cities*. We looked for those characters that best imitated Christ in their meekness, sacrifice, or charity. After Christians fell in love with *The Lord of the Rings*, they identified several characters as Christ figures: Aragorn the king, Gandalf who dies and is resurrected, the hobbits in their humility. In reality, the most lovely stories will show us thousands of reflections of Christ in the faces of dozens of characters. The truthfulness by which the authors depict the human beings in their work determines how much we will be able to see the Human One in the story. We should look for him everywhere.

However, I caution readers against two fallacies of reading with a biblical lens: first, prioritizing message over narrative, and second, so-called Christian literature that fronts as biblically informed.

As for the first, the Bible is mysterious and transcendent, so we should not reduce it to the level of Aesop's fables. Nor should we read a novel or poem and attempt to extract a message from it. I was being interviewed by a college provost once who continued to pester me to tell him what Flannery O'Connor's stories meant. As I persisted in talking about the narrative and its images, he pressed for me to give him a moral. O'Connor insisted that her stories could not be reduced to $x + y = z$. She writes, "A story really isn't any good unless it successfully resists paraphrase."[28] When we practice reading literature biblically, we should not walk away with bumper-sticker answers to what a story means.

As for the second warning, there are quite a few novels called "Christian" that rewrite Bible stories into historical fiction or romance. These stories tend to reduce the complexity of the biblical narrative to a simplistic tale for the easy digestion of readers. In their attempts to make the Bible palatable, they make God impotent. The author of Hebrews cautions the church against being satisfied with easy teachings, using the metaphor of an infant satisfied by milk: "Anyone who lives on milk . . . is not acquainted with the teaching about righteousness. But solid food is for the mature, who by constant use have trained themselves to distinguish good from evil" (Heb. 5:13–14). Perhaps the milk introduces the baby Christian to the faith, in the way that evangelical fiction might draw a nonbeliever into church. However, one should not be satisfied with such reading. All the mystery, grit, and challenge of the biblical story is anesthetized to suit contemporary readers' expectations. The question to ask is whether the reading calls you to be persistently kind to your enemies, to die to your selfish ambitions, to love what is beautiful, and so on. Do these books ask something of you? From my limited experience of reading evangelical fiction, our consciences will not be pricked by these books; these bestsellers often rub our egos, taste sweet, and sometimes turn us on in a way that feels safe. Instead, Christians should desire to read *literature* that trains us to distinguish good from evil—in a nuanced way—when we read our complicated world.

Humble Marginalia

When St. Augustine preached, he sat down, just as Jesus did in the Sermon on the Mount. Augustine opened the Bible in his lap, emphasizing the priority of the Word. This was not a fiery preacher with his hands in the air, his voice demanding and deafening. Rather, Augustine sat in his liturgical vestments before a crowd of African peasants who were hungry for God. Here is the emblem of a humble reader—with lowered posture and the pages inviting, the conversation begins. We see this posture in his exegetical writing as he asks questions and permits the mystery to transcend his limited reason. He converses with the text.

Some people find the idea of writing in a book blasphemous. It depends on the motivation with which you write. In a piece titled "A Weapon for Readers," Tim Parks describes scribbling in the margins "like a hawk over a field," as though the reader is a predator and the book is prey.[29] Such an approach will harm the writing and deform the reader. It is the posture that concerned Sontag when e-books became available. In *How to Read a Book*, Mortimer Adler writes of annotations as a way of owning the book: "Full ownership of a book comes only when you have made it a part of yourself, and the best way to make yourself a part of it . . . is by writing in it."[30] Although I cringe at the owning metaphor (how can anyone *own Moby-Dick* or *The Canterbury Tales*?), writing in the margins strengthens one's relationship to the book. The conversation morphs from a monologue into a dialogue. Also, Adler encourages readers to write in the margins that they might stay awake, be active thinkers, and remember well what they have read.

The poet Billy Collins relishes marginalia in his poem by that title. He contrasts the "ferocious" notes with the "offhand, dismissive—'Nonsense.'" Who has not stumbled on someone else's notes in a book and laughed at the cursory "No!" or "Yes!"

Better still are those personal comments, such as Collins records: "Don't be a ninny," which he found in *The Life of Emily Dickinson*.[31] These notes remind us that books are conversations between the author and the reader. Literature teachers instruct students how to mark tropes, repeated phrases, and connections between their current text and the ones they have read before. As Italo Calvino has reflected, books "come to us bearing the aura of previous interpretations, and trailing behind them the traces they have left in the culture."[32] It is not merely one person's conversation with a particular book—when we write "Plotinus" or "Virgil" in the margins of *Confessions*, we highlight that Augustine has had a conversation first with those authors through his book. Then we in turn converse with Jean-Jacques Rousseau and write "Augustine" in his margins (as much as the author would have hated for us to realize that he had a forerunner).

More than a studious enterprise, marking a text can be devotional. To circle a word or underline a sentence says, "I see you." By attending closely, you are practicing being a beholder. Collins ties our practice of marginalia to the Irish monks who

> jotted along the borders of the Gospels
> brief asides about the pains of copying,
> a bird singing near their window,
> or the sunlight that illuminated their page—
> anonymous men catching a ride into the future
> on a vessel more lasting than themselves.[33]

The monks attended to the text before them and recorded all the other beauties they beheld—birds and sunlight. By writing in the margins of these manuscripts, the monks testified to the long-lasting dialogue between books and their readers. When we write in our books, we join the ongoing conversation, we practice humility in a tangible way, and we engage the book with charity.

Addendum: Church Mothers

For the past few centuries, we have read primarily the church fathers, who were heavily influential in the early foundation of our faith, but we should not neglect the church mothers. Especially dear to me for their reading lives are fourth- and fifth-century monastics Melania the Elder and her granddaughter Melania the Younger. The Elder established the monastery on the Mount of Olives around the same time that St. Jerome was translating the Bible into Latin to make the Scriptures accessible to the common people. Misinformation causes us to imagine that Christians in the Roman Empire lacked a literary culture and that Martin Luther was the first to come up with the idea of a vulgar translation of the Bible.[34] In the fourth century, Melania the Elder was an avid reader. Her biographer Palladius concludes his hagiography by underscoring her reading life:

> She was most erudite and fond of literature, and she turned night into day going through every writing of the ancient commentators— three million lines of Origen and two and a half million lines of Gregory, Stephen, Pierius, Basil, and other worthy men. And she did not read them once only and in an offhand way, but she worked on them, dredging through each work seven or eight times. Thus it was possible for her to be liberated from *knowledge falsely so called* (1 Tim. 6:20) and to mount on wings, thanks to those books—by good hopes she transformed herself into a spiritual bird and so made the journey to Christ.[35]

Adhering to Augustine's example, Melania did not read casually, but with attention she returned repeatedly to the same books, filling her days with wholesome words. Her faithful reading habits liberated her from worldly ways of viewing things so she could ascend, as she always desired, to be finally with Christ.

Although Jerome complained that not enough women learned their Hebrew well enough to recite the Psalms in the original language, Melania the Younger consistently read not only the Hebrew Bible but also the Christian Scriptures in their entirety three to four times each year. Following her grandmother's example, she read and wrote regularly, as her biographer details: "[Melania] wrote elegantly and faultlessly in little notebooks. . . . After she had had her fill of these writings [canonical books and homilies], she went through the lives of the Fathers as if she were eating cake."[36] For her main entrée, Melania would begin with reading Scripture, then sermons, and then, for dessert, she relished the narratives of saints' lives. A woman who could have lived off her fortune—an inheritance some have calculated to exceed Kardashian dreams—gave up all her riches for the wealth of Christ. She traded the life of luxury for the feast of the Word.

3

What's the Difference between "Use" and "Enjoy"?

"God is useless," I wrote in blue marker across the whiteboard and turned to the dismayed and angry faces of two dozen college students. A hand shot up. Before I even called her name, the student began rattling off her protest like she was starring in the movie *God's Not Dead*.

"God may not be useful to you, but he is useful to me. I pray to him every day," she announced proudly, her earrings dangling to the beat of her words as she nodded her head in assurance of her own testimony.

"That is called 'idolatry,'" I responded. I relished too much that moment where my sweet student faltered. Here I was employing a religious term, and she thought I was challenging her faith. I continued to unpack what I meant.

"If you are *using* God, then you are treating him like an object. You are the subject. You are reigning over him and making him useful to your own purposes. Is that what you mean?"

Silence. Some jaws hung slightly open. Some eyes searched the ceiling for their thoughts. What I had challenged in my students was not their belief in God but their idol of use. They prized utility so much that they had even—unintentionally—conceived of God in terms of his usefulness to them. The reality is that God is useless. We humans cannot *use* God for any other thing than to be enjoyed. God is the end of all things. He is only to be enjoyed.

Augustine clarifies the distinction between "use" and "enjoy" in his manual on reading, *De Doctrina Christiana*. He writes,

> There are some things which are to be enjoyed, some which are to be used, and some whose function is both to enjoy and use. Those which are to be enjoyed make us happy; those which are to be used assist us and give us a boost, so to speak, as we press on towards our happiness, so that we may reach and hold fast to the things which make us happy.[1]

Augustine clarifies three categories rather than a dichotomy: things to enjoy (God alone), things to be used, and things to enjoy and use (books, people, and art, which lead to the enjoyment of God). When Augustine writes the word "happiness," he chooses the Latin verb *beāre*, from which we get our word "beatitude," or "blessed." "Happy is the one," begins Psalm 1—*Beatus vir* in Latin. The idea of happiness here points to blessedness, which extends beyond happenstance or mere pleasure. To receive joy like a grace is to be blessed. Enjoyment is the kind of happiness that Augustine intends. Through reading the Bible and other great art, one's capacity to love and enjoy God may increase.

We misuse literature when we *only* use it or when we use it for an end other than the enjoyment of God. Augustine explains, "To enjoy something is to hold fast to it in love for its own sake. To use something is to apply whatever it may be to the purpose of obtaining what you love."[2] In other words, God is to be loved for his own sake, not for the sake of anything that God may do for you. Other people are to be both enjoyed and used; you love them for the sake of God. Art, literature, and the Bible itself are to be used and enjoyed similarly, insofar as they point you to God.

The problem occurs when we denigrate things that are meant to be enjoyed and used for the enjoyment of God, such as people and art, to their mere usefulness. In our twenty-first-century culture, we neglect the real difference between "use" and "enjoy." We say "enjoy" when, in fact, we mean that we are *using* something—a book, movie, game—for our individual pleasure. We uplift to false heights the necessity of use. We want all things to be useful. Take reading or learning, for instance. We read a manual on car mechanics so we can fix a car. That kind of reading is solely useful. But we should not read Virgil's *Aeneid* in order that we may check a box on a great books list. Rather, a book such as the *Aeneid* is to be used—for pleasure and edification temporarily—and ultimately enjoyed in how it points us to God.

When we consider how we read or what we read, we should differentiate between the kinds of books that invite attention and rereading versus those that are for use—either solely for entertainment, solely for information, or solely for skills instruction. Reading as a spiritual discipline applies to those works of art that are to be, as Augustine writes, both used and enjoyed. Like a conversation with a good friend that draws out your love of God, a book can be used toward that end and enjoyed in that sense.

Why Enjoy a Good Book

Diane Glancy's poetic memoir, written in the voice of Ada Black-jack, begins with a line drawn between this woman who beholds the stars, those "polar lights," and the men who assess everything by merit of its use:

> The Polar Lights prowled like polar bears.
> The men watched the lights.
> What good were they?
> We could not hunt the lights.
> We could not eat them.[3]

In this fictional account based on a true story, we experience the real problem between these perspectives. Without an esteem for useless things, people miss what is beautiful. In the words of John Keats, "Beauty is truth, truth beauty."[4] The two transcendentals share the same source and point back to it—God. If we esteem only what is useful, what role does literature play in our lives? For reading fiction is useless unless it engenders the love of God. All imaginative works of beauty are useless in our modern conception of the word. But praise God for that.[5]

While stories or poems have transformative effects on their readers, heaven forbid they be *used* as such. In fact, one of the great reasons to read works of the imagination is to overcome our habitual disposition toward utility. Ever since John Stuart Mill, the modern founder of utilitarianism, suggested that utility was not merely trendy but necessary, we tend to assume that all our actions must be of use. We long to be busy and productive members of society.

But this is not our end. We are meant to be human beings, made in the image of a God who is Love, who is Beauty, who is Goodness, who is Truth. In an essay I regularly teach, "Why Should Businessmen Read Great Literature?" Vigen Guroian reminds us, "We are created to be principally lovers, not laborers."[6] We are made to love, first God and then neighbor. And indeed, by loving "whatever is true, whatever is noble, whatever is right, whatever is pure, whatever is lovely, whatever is admirable" (Phil. 4:8), we will better love God and neighbor.

For Christians, the hesitation to stock their shelves with fiction and poetry stems from a miscomprehension that conflates "imagination" with "illusion." Made-up things are not illusory, nor is fiction merely false. Is not this world governed by time, whereas we are eternal beings? And did not Jesus tell us stories that showed how upside down this world is, compared with his right-side-up kingdom? The devil prowls around unseen, but fiction, by describing the world as it is, unmasks him. No matter how covert the demonic operations, poetry undoes lies with truth. "Such power in the naming of things," goes Thomas Lynch's poem.[7]

We also suffer from a worldly sickness engineered by the Enlightenment project, a misapprehension of reason as the highest faculty and dislocated from our imagination. Such an assumption leads us to consider literature as unwarranted. *Novels and poems play with our emotions*, we think, *and clutter our pure reason*. But what if our emotions help us register our humanity, guiding us in moral decision-making? In *The Abolition of Man*, C. S. Lewis calls the heart or chest of the person, where we *feel* things, the "seat of magnanimity," where the humanity of the human being resides: "The head rules the belly through the chest—the seat, as [eleventh-century theologian] Alanus tells us, of Magnanimity, of emotions organized by trained habit into stable sentiments."[8] We are trained by great literature to correlate our feelings with the truth. To feel no pity at poverty is evidence of a desensitized imagination. To experience no joy when a soul has won a victory shows a lack of empathy, more signs of a poorly developed imagination.

In his excellent book *How to Think*, Alan Jacobs notes how even Mill was pulled from his depression by so-called useless poetry. Mill contemplates how William Wordsworth offered a balm for his soul, expressing "not mere outward beauty but states of feeling and of thought colored by feeling under the excitement of beauty."⁹ Poetry trained Mill in how to *feel* rightly. It was not enough that Mill had been taught the right principles, memorized the commandments, been catechized in true claims. He needed to love the beautiful and be drawn to the good. Jacobs writes, "To have your feelings moved by the beauty of a landscape is to respond to that landscape in the way that it deserves; to have your feelings moved in a very different direction by the sight of people living in abject poverty is to respond to *that* situation in the way that it deserves."¹⁰ Literature acts on the soul.

Our imaginations need such education because we are fallen, sinful creatures who easily become desensitized to evil. As Flannery O'Connor writes in one of her prayers, most of us have "lost the power to vomit" over sin, especially our own.¹¹ The most powerful stories are those that have us cast stones at our own reflections. To paraphrase O'Connor, they show us the devils that possess us—and hopefully help us exorcise them, by the grace of God.¹² In O'Connor's short story "Revelation," for instance, when the prideful Mrs. Ruby Turpin cries out at the Lord, Job-like, "Who do you think you are?" the question reverberates back over the field in an ominous echo.¹³ As readers, we hear the question addressed to us. *Yes*, we think—and hold our breath with Ruby—*who do we think we are?*

If we desire to know our Author, perhaps we should attend more to words, practicing reading and becoming better readers. In "As Kingfishers Catch Fire," Gerard Manley Hopkins writes, "Christ plays in ten thousand places."¹⁴ The poem lets us experience the gradient radiance of God's light, from the wings of a bird or dragonfly to the sounds of water falling over stones, and ultimately to the lovely limbs and eyes of our neighbor. The visceral reminders of beauty in this sonnet communicate a type of knowledge that cannot be conveyed with the same conviction by mere argument.

To Become a Beholder

I grew up in a home that prioritized reading. My father was a first-generation college student, and he majored in business to support his family. He allocated a portion of his monthly wages to the Book of the Month club through Easton Press. He and my mom would dine on bologna boats (mashed potatoes and cheese on fried bologna) so that he could afford to receive a great book in the mail each month. Those leather-bound copies with gilded pages made a strong impression on me as a kid. From those beautiful editions I read *The Adventures of Tom Sawyer*, *Walden*, *Jane Eyre*, and I knew—because of their beauty—they were a different sort of reading from my R. L. Stine paperback novels.

When we appreciate the beautiful, we are living up to our calling as beholders. Hopkins writes in "Hurrahing in Harvest," "These things were here and but the beholder / wanting."[15] Repeatedly in Scripture we are commanded to "behold." We are meant to delight in the beautiful and to cultivate beauty, as much as we are asked to know the true and to follow the good. These are not inseparable commands or hierarchical directives—the Good, the True, and the Beautiful all claim equal piety. We miss the mark when we cultivate ugliness, devalue beauty, or use beauty for our own satisfaction. Pop stations on the radio or dissonant advertising will anesthetize our senses; we will become people who cannot hear poetry or who do not love Duke Ellington. If we decry the fundraising for rebuilding Notre Dame Cathedral, we will become people who experience no tension when worshiping inside a YMCA or sending our children to schools that look like factory warehouses. As Christians, we are meant to love beautiful things, to visit art galleries, to desire aesthetically pleasing buildings, to stand still before the sunset.

Reading beautiful literature increases our capacity to behold, to pay attention in order to see, and to enjoy useless goods.[16] We love the most useless things. To say God is useless, then, as I began, is not to say that God does not matter, but the opposite. God matters most: he is the end and thus cannot be *used* for anything. Beauty turns us away from the sin of prioritizing use and reminds us to enjoy. When we consider our chief end as human beings, is it not, after all, "to glorify God and to *enjoy* him forever"?[17] From where does this enjoyment come but from the beauty of God?

How to Enjoy a Good Book

In *An Experiment in Criticism*, C. S. Lewis writes, "The many *use* art and the few *receive* it."[18] Once we confront our idol of use, we can approach the art before us with gratitude, ready to receive a gift. We should approach a text as we approach a person. In the same way that we should see a person as an end rather than a means, so should we love a book. For Lewis, if we assume a text is full of errors prior to reading it, we will probably find all the fallacies we had thought were there all along. But if we begin by assuming a piece of writing is good, we may discover "we were paying the author an undeserved compliment"[19]—or we may find an unexpected trove of wisdom. You must remove your biases and expectations. Lewis writes, "The first demand any work of art makes upon us is surrender. Look. Listen. Receive. Get yourself out of the way."[20] To many readers, the idea of removing prejudice seems impossible: How can I get myself out of the way of my reading? Not to mention that such a request may seem too frightening. Without healthy skepticism, we could be taken advantage of. If we surrender to a work, we become vulnerable. The author would have the power to oppress us.

There are many reasons we may approach a book with preconceived notions or hurdles of self that we struggle to overcome. If a book is recommended to you by someone you trust or admire, you may assume the book possesses an authority that it does not deserve. When I have taught contentious texts, like Nietzsche's

Beyond Good and Evil, I find students grappling with the reading because they cannot align their respect for my judgment with their discomfort with the author. I do not assign only books that I agree with; I regularly recommend books about which I have strong reservations regarding the author's point of view or argument. I'm a firm believer in reading works that challenge our assumptions and pull off the snuggly blanket. When reading, we must not assume the book will be good or bad based on who approves or disapproves of it. We can no more read Flannery O'Connor's short stories with our guard up because someone accused her of being racist than we can dislike Philip Pullman's novels because we heard he was an atheist. Read the work and consider it on its own merits. To read with uncritical embrace or undue criticism increases factionalism rather than encouraging interdependent thinking.

In addition to those external reviews of books that may lead us to be critical or accepting without reason, consider your personal prejudices about what you assume renders a book great. I've eavesdropped on conversations at coffee shops where people have asserted baldly, "I don't like reading women writers—they are so fluffy and touchy-feely." Imagine if you said such aspersions against women in general: "I don't want that person at my dinner party because women are so emotional." No one would stand for it. (Or at least I hope they wouldn't!) Personally, I hated *Billy Budd* when I read it in high school. I was a teenager. It was poorly taught. And I bet someone chose it because it's one of Melville's shorter novels, without considering how high school readers would take the story. Melville made a lame first impression on me, which kept me from reading *Moby-Dick* for years. When I finally picked up the novel in my late twenties, I loved it so much that I read it twice in succession. We have to admit what our prejudices are, examine on what they are based, and then lay them aside so we can enjoy the book before us.

These kinds of prejudices hinder relationships in the church too. Some Christians are less willing to accept the sinner who curses or wears inappropriate clothing, despite the viciousness in every heart that we seem to allow or ignore. So with books: we cannot condemn a book because it uses foul language. I have grown red in the face at thoughtless readers censoring *The Tale of Despereaux*, a beautiful and heroic children's novel, because a mouse says, "*Mon Dieu!*" Instead of blatant disregard, readers have to ask, "Who said the vulgar words? Why? What does it tell us about his or her character? Is the use of such language being uplifted by the author? Does the author want you to feel the grit of such words in opposition to the beauty elsewhere in the narrative?" And so on. I am more offended by books that lie to readers or exalt villains as heroes or misuse the English language than I am about "bad" words. Charles Dickens said somewhere that there's no substitute for a "well-placed 'damn.'" While you may not want to wear a T-shirt that fronts "I'm Christian and I curse sometimes," we need to see beyond superficial barriers to judge the virtue or viciousness of the work, which does include its language.

Of course, some readers cannot move past these hurdles. Reading is a lifelong journey, just as sanctification or education is. Whether twenty years old or sixty years old, we may not be ready to read George Saunders or Kurt Vonnegut because we cannot see past their vulgarity. Our tastes have to be cultivated—not immunized—and this process requires time and practice as readers. My husband cannot read books in which children die without it burdening him for months on end. He detests Dante's *Inferno* because of the gore. These are not marks of vice. In Paul's argument with the Corinthians, he refutes their claim that "I have the right to do anything" by reminding them, "Not everything is beneficial" (1 Cor. 10:23). Although I defend authors' use of coarse diction for certain effects, not every reader needs to subject herself to it. You do not have to enjoy Percival

Everett's or Walker Percy's novels (filled as they are with foul language) to be a good reader.

Love of God and Love of Neighbor

If we are to read spiritually, we must begin by loving books in a similar fashion to loving our neighbors, seeing the book as an opportunity to practice charity. Simone Weil writes, "Not only does the love of God have attention for its substance; the love of our neighbour, which we know to be the same love, is made of this same substance."[21] In his *Poetics*, Aristotle explains that literature provides vicarious experience for the viewer in the case of theater, or reader in the case of poetry and fiction. We feel the fear or pity or elation through our reading of the text. Thousands of years later, cognitive science confirms the truth of Aristotle's observations.[22] This is why literary theorists treat reading as a way of building empathy. In reality, reading can be a resource for the pious reader to cultivate understanding of other perspectives, other times and places, other griefs or joys than what she has encountered in her life. What these truths mean for the spiritual reader is that reading may be a practice that increases our capacity to love. If we open ourselves to the love of our neighbor in the book before us, we may gain in charity through the gift of reading. If we move from instrumentalizing books to enjoying them, we may find we have more means with which to love and enjoy God.

4

Do Good Books Make You a Good Person?

ad people have read good books. I'm not sure why that should be surprising, unless you believe that good books have a magical ability to transform sinners into saints. What is illogical is to cast aside good books as though they are bad because their readers are not as good as those books. On social media, you'll encounter contrarians to reading who argue that the Founding Fathers were classically educated, but since they owned slaves, their education was worthless. Or because soldiers quoted Homer in the midst of World War I, the classics are no defense against violence. I struggle to take these arguments seriously. Why should we assume any salvific power in literature? To me, the more interesting question is the assumption itself: What does it say about literature that people *assume* its ability to transfigure us?

Reading books will not save your soul. It will not transform a bad person into a good one (though books might convert a boring person into someone more interesting). We do not read books to stave off the apocalypse or to hold our heads high above those silly nonreaders. There should be no political agenda or selfish ambition to reading. Rather, reading is a spiritual discipline akin to fasting and prayer and one that trains you in the virtues, encourages your sanctification, and elicits your love for those noble, admirable, and beautiful things of which St. Paul writes in his Letter to the Philippians. We read because without books our world shrinks, our empathy thins, and our liberty wanes. We read for the same reason that people have read—and shared poems or stories—for thousands of years: because our eyes are not enough by which to see. The time and place in which we live blinds us to other perspectives and ways of being that are not of our own experience. We read because we have been given the gift of imagination and intellect, and we exhibit our gratitude by using it.

In Defense of Reading

In the twelfth century, Marie de France counseled the courts of Henry II of England and his wife Eleanor of Aquitaine to continue reading the great stories and passing them on. In the preface to her medieval *lais*, which are small poems that parody courtly love, Marie writes, "Anyone who has received from God the gift of knowledge and true eloquence has a duty not to remain silent: rather should one be happy to reveal such talents. When a truly beneficial thing is heard by many people, it then enjoys its first blossom."[1] Marie charges us with the duty to bring these good things to life by reading them. Words remain lifeless until a reader engages them. Before Marie begins to relay her stories, she credits their inspiration to ancient tales that she has taken on the responsibility of retelling. If the stories are worth knowing, we have to share them, else they lie as fallow seeds in the earth. For Marie, readers have as much responsibility as writers for remembering the good, true, and beautiful and passing them on.

"It is not fitting that such understanding and intellectual power as you possess were given you in vain, not fitting that you should be satisfied with mediocrity; such gifts expect and encourage the highest excellence."[2] This exhortation sounds like it may have come from a professor to a student. If I told you these words were written in the 1400s, you might assume it was the direction of a master scholar to his apprentice, a young man with opportunities to serve his city. However, this is the admonition given by Leonardo Bruni, the chancellor of Florence, a forerunner in civic humanism, to Battista Malatesta, a forty-year-old widow with daughters and granddaughters, whom she desired to raise up according to the ideals of liberal education in spite of society's distaste for women's education. Malatesta was a grandniece of the famous Montefeltros (who are mentioned in Dante's *Divine Comedy*); she herself became a scholar and public orator of great renown. In fact, during her time, there is record of a wedding oration in which a father says, "Our time is not lacking in outstanding women who deserve praise. . . . Who has not heard of Battista Malatesta?"[3]

Bruni advises Malatesta, a woman who had no leading role in her society, a woman who could never be chancellor or a professor or have any mercenary or vocational use for her studies of literature, to dedicate herself to an education in great books. Why? In order to show gratitude for the gift of intellect that she had received. Too many young men in his day were disdaining liberal education, which he found shameful, and turning out clumsy rhetoric. Bruni provides Malatesta with a great books list that starts with the Bible and the church fathers and then adds all the great poets up to their day—Homer, Virgil, Augustine, Hesiod, Boethius, Cicero, and others. Because of her studies, when opportune moments came, Malatesta found herself addressing the future Holy Roman emperor, as well as the pope, then subsequently educating her daughters and granddaughters, who also gained a reputation in their time for civic leadership.

We see in Marie and in Malatesta the necessity of reading, that the practice of reading is a responsibility.

Vicious Habits of Reading

No matter what you read, if you read without virtue you cannot read well. A maniacal deviant reading the Bible will only find heresies. How can an arrogant and vicious person enjoy something as spiritually resonant as *The Divine Comedy* or *Paradise Lost*? While both Mother Teresa and Hitler may have read the *Aeneid*, they could not have gleaned the same beauty, truth, or goodness from the epic. Just as an impatient glassmaker will never turn out a lovely vase or a cowardly chef will never surpass crafting basic camp-food fare, so too a vicious reader will never understand why people enjoy books so much. With nary a peep of protest, these readers may throw out all but thirty of their unbeloved books.

For half a century, literary critic Harold Bloom taught people to read without virtue. Bloom pictures readers *against* the texts and their authors. Interpretation is "the exercise of the Will-to-Power *over* texts," he writes, explicitly aligning himself with Friedrich Nietzsche.[4] To be a "strong" reader, one *must* misread a text. If you try to understand the author, they have mastery over you. If you attend to the text, it influences you and thus it wins. From Bloom's perspective, which has subtly influenced literature departments—and therefore students—for fifty-odd years, the idea that a text has spiritual significance is an illusion: "The sad truth is that poems don't have presence, unity, form, or meaning. Presence is a faith, unity is a mistake or even a lie, form is a metaphor, and meaning is an arbitrary and now repetitious metaphysics."[5] Because, for Bloom, all our relationships between text, author, and reader are illusory, we should purposefully misread the text and thus make our own meaning from our encounter with the book.

Few readers are as intentionally unvirtuous readers as Bloom; in fact, most readers probably do not recognize that they may be practicing more vice than virtue in their reading. We may convince ourselves that a book means something that goes against all the evidence to the contrary. Readers have decried Homer as a white supremacist, not realizing how alien the idea of race would have been for the ancient poet. Having suffered trauma or mourning or deep grief, readers may be sensitive to images within a text and walk away bruised or singed by an author who never intended any such response. Although you may be a courageous person on the football field or a mama bear to your children, are you dauntless in your choice of reading? Do you approve of op-eds that censor and demand cutting books from libraries? Or do you laugh in the face of "dangerous" authors such as Mary Wollstonecraft, Jean-Paul Sartre, or Christopher Hitchens? We must each overcome our readerly vices and not be a too "timid friend of truth" in our choice of books.[6] Nor should we be unjust toward writers and judge their work too quickly or unfairly.

Spiritual Reading

To approach the activity of reading as a discipline requiring virtue, one should read spiritually. On top of *spiritual* reading, we could employ a host of other adjectives to modify reading, such as "active reading" or "slow reading." Mortimer Adler coaches us in *How to Read a Book* to become "demanding" readers who are alert and engaged in the reading activity.[7] David Mikics trains us to become "slow" readers, so we don't merely process books like we're devouring fast-food meals.[8] I want to promote "spiritual reading" because, as Georges Bernanos writes, "grace is everywhere."[9] Or, as St. Paul writes, "Whether you eat or drink [or read great literature], do it all for the glory of God" (1 Cor. 10:31). Everything that Christians do should be spiritual.

For the early church theologians, virtue was the precursor and by-product of spiritual reading. "Any interpretation that does not lead to growth in virtuous habits is, according to patristic exegesis, not interpretation that is worthy of God," theologian Hans Boersma writes.[10] Granted, the church fathers were only concerned with the virtues instilled in readers by their encounter with Scripture. Not every book you read will train you in moral virtue. However, if you read spiritually, you will be seeking out these goods; you will be practicing spiritual virtues in your efforts to understand the author, seek the good in the text, and love the book for what it is.

I could write a dozen books on being a hospitable reader, courageous reader, just reader. For the early church exegetes, the virtues repeatedly exalted for a reader included humility, hospitality, and charity. So many of the virtues bleed into one another—they are more like currents within a river than separate streams. Of course, the catch-22 is that one must be a virtuous reader to become more virtuous by the process of reading. Although it is paradoxical, it is nonetheless true: To receive the gifts that reading offers, one must approach reading as a gift.

BOOKMARK 2

———•———

Reading like Julian of Norwich

Through her *Revelations of Divine Love,* Julian of Norwich tests our knowledge of what it means to live what we read and to share our journey with others. The author who we call Julian of Norwich was an anchoress who resided in the city of Norwich, walled into the cathedral known as St. Julian's Church. Her anonymity was the norm for medieval authors, especially women. (The name of the author Marie de France, for instance, merely means "Mary from France.") Her revelations make up the first English book written by a woman. Like Dante, whose *Divine Comedy* had popularized writing poetry in the vernacular for Italians, or Chaucer, whose *Canterbury Tales* were written in English vernacular, so Julian breaks down the barriers to theology by writing in the common speech of everyday people.

Sister Julia Bolton Holloway opens her book on Julian by expressing frustration with all those scholars who say, "Very little is known about the Anchoress Julian of Norwich," for if you read Julian's work closely, the author tells you about not only her inner life but also many facts about herself. Women such as Christine de Pizan, Elizabeth Barrett Browning, or Julian of

Norwich "are best portrayed in their books, in manuscript, in print, and in whole libraries, shelving their books."[1] Drawing from a close reading of *Revelations*, Holloway contends that Julian may have been a *conversi*, a member of a Jewish family forced by the king of England's 1290 edict that demanded Jews convert or be expelled. Although not educated in Latin or the biblical languages, for no women were permitted formal education in the fourteenth century, Julian seems to be translating passages of Scripture into Middle English in what she calls her "showings."[2] In addition to her knowledge of the Word, Julian may have taught schoolchildren through the window of her anchor-hold, and we know she counseled pilgrims and locals who visited her.[3]

Julian lived through the Black Death as a young girl. At the age of thirty, she suffered what was thought to be a fatal illness and received last rites from a priest. During this near-death experience, Julian received visions from God. After she recovered, Julian wrote down these revelations and began to unpack their meaning. Holloway has found a manuscript dated 1386 of the showings, and the latest version, called "The Long Text," may have been completed between 1410 and 1420. In between these dates, John Wycliffe was declared a heretic for his English translation of the Bible, so the second manuscript lacks the biblical sources found plentifully in the 1386 version. Because of her many descriptions of motherhood, scholars believe she was a mother before she became an anchoress.

The life of an anchoress (or anchorite) was not an abnormal way of expressing piety; there were more than a hundred in England during the fourteenth century. These recluses chose to be walled up in a cell attached to the cathedral, where they could see the altar and thus experience regular Mass, as well as have a window to the outside world and care for the needs of their community. In the early thirteenth century, there was even a guidebook for anchoresses so one could perform the vocation well.[4] For Julian, the life in the anchor-hold provided space to work on her showings and their interpretation. She spent nearly four decades repeatedly reading, meditating on, and interpreting her showings. Reading this medieval author helps us imagine different ways of reading than our culture prescribes.

Glossing the Text

With her revelations, Julian is not adding to the authoritative Scripture, but like the monks who explicated the Bible with commentary, Julian glosses Scripture with her showings. The *Glossa Ordinaria* was a collection of organized commentary on the Bible—mostly drawn from church fathers—that explained difficult passages. Today, we might consider "glossing" synonymous with "annotating." When we write in the margins of our books for ourselves and make notes, we gloss. In the prologue to her *lais*, Marie de France writes, "It was customary for the ancients, in the books which they wrote . . . to express themselves very obscurely so that those in the later generations, who had to learn them, could provide a gloss for the text and put the finishing touches to their meaning."[5] Marie points out that glossing distills the mystery and highlights the meaning of the text. It allows other readers to join the conversation.

If you look at the *Glossa Ordinaria*, it is difficult to unthread the Scripture from the commentary, for all the text together composes the tapestry on the page. Similarly, medieval writers such as Julian would not have considered it necessary to untangle Scripture from its interpretation. Hugh of St. Victor, for example, includes the church fathers with the New Testament in his definition of "Scripture." He also lists the writings and acts of the popes all the way up to his day. "The implication is that all these people and events are signs which have a status equivalent to scriptural history."[6] Imagine Scripture and its interpretation in the life of the church as a marriage, where the two become one, yet they each have a separate identity. We would not have the New Testament had not Jesus fulfilled the Old Testament in his life, and the apostles then interpreted the Old Testament in letters and acts of their own. Or the revelations of John, which rely not only on the Old and New Testaments but also on the contemporary cities and churches to which he refers. John's revelations also receive interpretation prophetically throughout the history of the church, coming to life again each time they are read in a new era. The Bible itself would not have been canonized without the interpretation and mediation of the church, and we would not be reading it in English without the various translators rewriting it into new languages and living forms. Words live within a community of readers, and Julian shows us this way of understanding texts more vitally than perhaps our culture is accustomed to.

When Julian is shown something, she applies the word "see" both to that vision and to the interpretation of it. For Julian, the showing and its gloss possess the same significance. Denys Turner notes how Julian's writing "does indeed parallel the practice of the medieval exegete, who would have found it quite implausible to draw any sharp distinction between the biblical text as a primary datum of revelation and the Church's practices of that text's reception, as if either had any authority independently of the other."[7] For example, the Lord shows Julian "a little thing, the size of a hazel-nut in the palm of my hand, and it was as round as a ball." Julian stares at the object with her "mind's eye" and asks, "What can this be?" To which she receives an answer from outside herself: "It is all that is made." The dialogue with God continues in her mind. She wonders how such a thing could last, and her mind answers, "It lasts and will last forever because God loves it; and everything exists in the same way by the love of God."[8] Through a dialogic approach to the text, Julian shows us how to interact with what we read. Just as Julian clarifies her vision of the hazelnut through a conversation, glossing brings another's words to life within the reader.

Imitatio Julian

On the *Holy Post* podcast, one of the hosts, Christian Taylor, was wondering why, when she looks back at pictures of herself from high school, she resembles Belinda Carlisle: they did their hair the same way, wore the same earrings and similar clothes, and so on.[9] Yet they didn't even know each other. Could it be that Christian's love for the Go-Go's translated into her imitation of the lead singer? How much are we affected by the culture we consume? This is a minor and humorous example of imitation that nonetheless indicates something deeply and universally true about human nature: we are imitators. Our very design is in the image of another, and our telos is to imitate his likeness. That process is encouraged or hindered by what we watch, listen to, and, of course, read.

To imitate what you read is a form of tropological reading, which we will unpack in more detail in chapter 6. A tropological reader interprets the book in how she lives a text. She does not merely process the words and then forget them, but she becomes in action what she has read. While we participate in tropological interpretation all the time, we rarely put that label on it, nor do we stop and consider why or how to read tropologically with purpose and intent. After all, without purpose and intent, we might imitate negative examples without recognizing their influence over our decisions. On the upside, in the medieval understanding, tropology was more than parroting a text; it could be "participation in the divine life."[10]

In *Revelations*, Julian assumes that her showings are not meant for her alone; rather, by sharing them, they achieve their full purpose. She writes, "I am not good because of the showing unless I love God better; and if you love God better, it is meant more for you than for me."[11] The medievalist Barbara Newman explains, "Such shifts between the individual and the universal occur because the medieval 'I' is anchored in a relationship of the self to itself that is unfamiliar to us. This 'I' presupposes a universal [Person] who dwells within each individual."[12] Julian imagines herself not as an individual recipient of these visions but as a person within a larger body of others who all desire God to reveal himself.

Aware of her readers, Julian desires that she—as well as they—respond to the showings by changing how she lives—and how they live. The showings are intended to teach people how to seek God, read the world, and know the self. Julian says explicitly that her visions came that "I may learn to know myself and reverently fear my God."[13] Holloway writes, "Julian presents us with herself, mirroring us, her readers, and what she is holding in her hand, as we hold in our hands her book, is a simple, small thing, the size of a natural hazel nut, as in a homely cookbook, the 'quantity' of a hazel nut, hand, hazel nut, book, these objects codifying all that God has made."[14] We are meant to experience the revelation with Julian and then turn to our world and see God continually revealing himself there.

For anyone who wants to be moved to love the good and hate the evil, Julian points them to the Lord, who answers in parables and revelations. Her way of reading Scripture and her revelations did not end in decoding the words but was fulfilled in her life as a contemplative in the anchor-hold. Theologian Donyelle McCray calls Julian's life a "sermon." "Her faith performance," McCray writes, "traversed the boundary between public and private and her inner life became a public profession of Christ's death and resurrection."[15] As an anchoress reading and meditating daily on these revelations, Julian put into action what she had read. She writes, "We are enclosed in the Father, and we are enclosed in the Son, and we are enclosed in the Holy Ghost. And the Father is enclosed in us, and the Son is enclosed in us, and the Holy Ghost is enclosed in us."[16] For Julian, these words were not merely spiritual but also physically experienced in a walled-up enclosure. Julian lives out the words that she writes, showing us dramatically what it means to "be endlessly borne, and never come out of Him" who is our "Saviour [and] our Very Mother."[17] Her example is a tropological reading of her interpretation of Scripture.

Living as an anchoress, Julian imitates the way that prophets performed their sermons in the Old Testament. We cannot forget Ezekiel lying on his side and cooking over dung. Or Hosea marrying the prostitute repeatedly and naming his children after God's messages. McCray describes Julian's life as "an icon facilitating divine encounter. And, in pointing to Christ rather than herself, the anchoress followed the model of John the Baptist, who sought Christ's glory rather than his own."[18] By acting out the text that she read, then writing imaginative revelations in response to her encounter with the Word, Julian models for readers how to read tropologically. Christians read for pleasure, but they also read to live in imitation of Christ. "The purpose of the Word," David Lyle Jeffrey emphasizes, "is not finally a matter of words, but is an embodying deed in the Person who by so faithful a reading 'becomes' the Word."[19] We are to live out what we have read.

"Tropology is enacted in love," writes Ryan McDermott.[20] And that is the ultimate message of Julian's *Revelations of Divine Love*. After fifteen years of meditating on her revelations, Julian receives an answer as to what they mean: "Do you want to know what our Lord meant? Know well that love was what he meant. Who showed you this? Love. What did he show? Love. Why did he show it to you? For love. Hold fast to this and you will know and understand more of the same; but you will never understand or know from it anything else for all eternity."[21] Julian did not leap to this exegesis; she waited patiently for an answer to her questions, closely investigating her visions, ruminating on them for years. Rather than respond in ecstasy as some mystics might, Julian analyzes her visions, numbering the responses, being as systematic as possible. And yet, the conclusion of such study is Love. Without an interpretation that begets an increase in charity, reading is meaningless.

Multiple Meanings of a Text

In *Confessions*, Augustine posits that Scripture may possess a multiplicity of meaning. He seeks God's wisdom on interpretation, addressing him in prayer: "As long as each interpreter is endeavoring to find in the holy scriptures the meaning of the author who wrote it, what evil is it if an exegesis he gives is one shown to be true by You, light of all sincere souls, even if the author whom he is reading did not have that idea and, though he had grasped a truth, had not discerned that seen by the interpreter?"[22] In other words, interpreters who desire to know God through their reading may perceive a truth beyond what the human author intended.

Julian elucidates further why one text may possess such a variety of interpretations. For Julian, if love is the meaning and love can be enacted in a variety of lived responses over time and place, then a text overflows with ways of meaning. We must overcome the desire to solve the mystery, to have one solution, to answer the miniature English teacher inside us that keeps demanding, "What does it mean?" If "love" is what it means, then Julian's words become a chorus for us, a song that we do not want to get out of our heads, and one that we can practice intentionally living, as she herself illustrates. Julian shows that textual interpretation is more than a game of deciphering codes; reading precipitates a perpetual cycle of lives in which the meaning is made incarnate. Julian concludes, "This book was begun by God's gift and his grace, but it seems to me that it is not yet completed."[23] The disciple John says of Jesus's life that there are not enough pages in the world to write down everything he did. In that sense, his Gospel is only partial, for Jesus continues to be manifest and move in all of us readers. So, too, Julian insinuates that the work God began through revelations to her is not finished simply because she ceases in writing about them; they have further life in her readers.

While readers may be uncomfortable with mystery, Julian indicates that readers need not know everything there is to know. The words "revelations" and "showings" in Julian's title may lead us to believe that Julian's visions will be clear, whereas we find that they are confounding and that the Lord has concealed from her and us as much as he has seemed to reveal. She explains that we will know all that is needful, but that some utterances exceed her wit, are not fully explained, and are meant to be "hidden and closed."[24] Reading literature will not produce all the answers, for the greatest of stories require a lifetime of rereading, just as Julian shows in her dedication to unpacking her visions. In a world where we are taught there are no limits to our knowledge, Julian's *Revelations* offer a beautiful antidote. We see that reading should humble us and delight us with its mystery. We do not have to have all the answers.

Women Writers

If one has eyes to see, the Middle Ages were brimming with exegesis authored by women.[25] However, most textbooks or histories, even the *Introduction to Medieval Theology* published by Cambridge University Press in 2012, for instance, leave women entirely out of the story. While you could not visit a church or cathedral during the eleventh to fifteenth centuries without seeing the visages of holy women in frescoes or stained glass, the last few hundred years of theology seem to have cut these women from the picture. Medieval women, however, contributed to a movement away from the scholastic approach to Scripture and toward the devotional; they wrote about God in a way that was personal, in the vernacular, and that drew on images from everyday life. They were the ones schooling the children in how to read, bringing up the future church, and passing on the tradition. If we do not look at how women read Scripture, what stories they read and told, or how they practiced living out their reading, we're missing half the narrative.

In the early part of the twentieth century, Dorothy L. Sayers was an anomaly for her time, not only because she earned her own income but also because she—a *woman*—was a translator, a writer, and a lay theologian. She defends the privilege of the scholarly and contemplative life for women in a 1938 talk titled "Are Women Human?" With her characteristic wit, Sayers calls out the church for not endorsing God's opinion on the matter: "I have never heard a sermon preached on the story of Mary and Martha that did not attempt . . . to explain away its text. . . . Martha was doing a really feminine job, whereas Mary was just behaving like any other disciple, male or female; and that is a hard pill to swallow."[26] Although Sayers stands apart from twentieth-century Protestant culture in her exposition of Luke 10, she maintains a perspective that was repeated throughout the tradition about women and their call to be contemplatives.

Like Mary who sat at Jesus's feet to hear his words, the Mother of God is depicted in church art as one who pored over the Word. She is shown engrossed in a book when the angel suddenly appears to announce her status as the Mother of God. Scholar Laura Saetveit Miles documents "thousands of manuscript illuminations, altar paintings, sculptures, relief carvings, rood screens, wall paintings, stained glass, textiles and pilgrim badges [that] depict the Annunciation scene . . . Gabriel flying in, Mary with her book."[27] Miles highlights the necessity of showing Mary as a reader: "Because the Virgin saw herself reflected in the virgin of Isaiah's prophecy, medieval readers could see themselves reflected in their books, whether that was the Bible, retellings of the Bible, or other devotional texts."[28] This image of Mary as a reader becomes foundational not only as an icon for female literacy but more significantly as the exemplar of a believer. Whether you are male or female, Christ's life in you begins with knowing the Word.

Unlike their male counterparts, Jesus's female disciples recognized the countercultural move occurring for women in Jesus's ministry. Sayers notes how different Jesus appeared to these women who were used to hearing nagging, flattering, coaxing, or patronizing words from men. "Perhaps it is no wonder," Sayers writes, "that the women were first at the Cradle and last at the Cross. They had never known a Man like this." For Jesus, there was never "anything 'funny' about woman's nature."[29] They could learn at his feet as well as a man; they could go and spread the word about him, as in the garden by his tomb he instructed Mary Magdalene.

In the short version of her showings, Julian asks, "Just because I am a woman, must I therefore believe that I must not tell you about the goodness of God, when I saw at the same time both his goodness and his wish that it should be known?"[30] When I shared this quote on social media, a man retorted, "Has this ever been debated?" I responded by relating how my male students have turned me in to my supervisor because I was talking about God in class, and it was not right for a woman to speak on such things (even if that woman has a PhD in theology). Or when I was a young girl, the elders of a church reprimanded me for singing louder than the men during worship. Yes, we too often stop women from sharing the goodness of God. At the time of Julian, she could have been burned at the stake—the punishment for heresy in England—for, as the chancellor of Paris Jean Gerson writes, "The female sex is forbidden on apostolic authority to teach in public . . . because it is not proved that they are witness to divine grace."[31] Julian risked her life to share what she had learned about God, not allowing these threats to silence her. At first, she apologizes for being a woman, calling herself "ignorant, weak, and frail."[32] However, in the longer version of the text, written decades later, Julian does not make any excuses for her sex.

As a woman, Julian did not suffer from the a priori assumptions or theological education that may have locked her male contemporaries within certain paradigms. She could play more, personalize without fear, and thus be an author with greater versatility and innovation than those who in the schools were taught certain ways to think and read. Welcomed into the canon more over the past few decades, Julian's *Revelations of Divine Love* counteract a narrative that insists that only men have been exegetes in church history, only men have succeeded in writing beautiful works of literature, or only men have preached with divine authority. Her book as much as her life testifies to the broader invitation by Jesus Christ to study at his feet. The contemplative life was not closed to women, and Julian's work reminds twenty-first-century women that such a life remains open to them. With Julian, we learn how to read the Bible outside of a monolithic perspective. Hopefully, through the literary gift of this woman, we learn the meaning of love.

5

What Does the Trinity Have to Do with the ART of Reading?

Years ago, I attended a faculty development session led by a literature professor. All the faculty of the university attended, no matter their discipline. Business professors in their matching polos with department insignia sat next to nursing professors in scrubs. The leader of the session assigned each table a piece of flash fiction and one poem. We read the literature at our tables, discussed it in disparate groups, and then the conversation opened up broadly to the whole room. As a humanities professor, I was floored by some of my colleagues' ineptness at interpreting fiction. These were PhDs who should have been able to process succinct passages of literature at a decent level. Instead, the stories were manipulated and misunderstood, and then those grievous interpretations defended. The poor reading of the poem was perhaps more egregious. You could tell that some of them had not read a poem in decades. I wondered how their inexperience with poetry affected their reading of the Psalms. Of Isaiah's prophecy or Daniel's visions. As one colleague asserted, "I can make it mean whatever I want." Is this how these professors at a Christian university were also handling Scripture? Could they make such apologies in defense of their personal interpretations of the Word of God?

Splitting Up the Trinity

When I teach literature courses, I dedicate a good amount of time to correcting false assumptions about reading, showing students instead what ideal reading should look like, and lifting their practices higher to that of spiritual reading. Rather than walk through the history of literary criticism—a fun but unnecessary romp through our shared timeline—let's take a look at where we are now. One can enter a literature classroom and spend fifty minutes trying to figure out what book or author the students are purportedly reading. In place of the author and text, you will hear about the critics—Jacques Derrida, Henry Louis Gates Jr., Julia Kristeva, or Karl Marx. You may hear a bunch of nonsense about what the students feel, what they liked or didn't like. If you watch a few episodes of *The Chair*, a Netflix show about an English department, you'll get a sense of what I mean: the students discuss white supremacy in *Moby-Dick* or insult Chaucer because he's boring. The problem began when we separated author from reader from text. Posed against one another, these three aspects of the reading experience fought for primacy in the reading activity. Literary critics stepped up and determined which had authority over the others—author, reader, or text. In place of balanced interpretation, we compose one-sided and heavy-handed fallacies—we only *use* rather than *use and enjoy* what is before us.

In that aforementioned faculty conversation, the professor who claimed that she could make the text mean whatever she wanted it to mean was assuming the preeminence of the reader in interpreting the meaning of a text. In the 1980s, critic Stanley Fish led the charge for these ideas with his reader-response theory.[1] According to Fish, the text does not have meaning apart from that assigned by the reader. Rather, the words lie dead on the page until the reader reads them, then they are breathed to life by the reader, and thus *made* by the reader. Fish prioritizes the reader in the meaning-making relationship with the text. "If all is in the reader," writes my former teacher Stephen Prickett, "all is relative, all is equal. A laundry-list is no different from literature."[2] The effect of this theory has led teachers to ask, "What does Toni Morrison's story make you feel?" Or "Which part of Dante's journey do you like better—Inferno, Purgatory, or Paradise?" Those are not invalid questions, but are they the only questions? Are they the primary questions?

After years of experiencing this reader-centered teaching—which likely started when we were very young—we assume our right to determine the worth of a piece of literature based on our response to it. People chuck their copy of *The Violent Bear It Away* because it made no sense to them. Or they declare that *Don Quixote* is a waste of time because they did not like it. Instead of discovering meaning within the text, in this method of reading, the work of art has value only if *we* grant it value. Using reader-response theory, a person insists that others cannot argue with her subjective experience of the text. Unfortunately, this way of reading also leads readers to look for themselves within the text. In order for a book to be meaningful, they must see themselves in it, often not in a deeply human way. They want to see their demographic represented, rather than human nature universally explored. Readers practice a way of reading that prioritizes texts with which they agree, that make readers feel good, but that way of reading does not ask anything from the readers that they are not willing to give.

The next attack on the reading experience came when we objectified the book or poem, placing it beneath a microscope, or worse, taking it apart like scientists disassembling a cadaver. The ways of destroying a text are legion. One possibility—we fall for deconstructionism and play with the endless meaning of the words until the words mean nothing. Or we assume that the text is all-encompassing, apart from its writer or reader, locating all meaning exclusively within its words. In either assumption, we undervalue or overvalue the words before us. Even those with good intentions, those who want to exalt the text and love the words before them, catalyze misinterpretations by ignoring the other elements in the reading experience. Be wary of interpretations that do not provide equal weight to reader, text, and author.

In grade school, we likely learned these various ways of deciphering books. Most of us were quizzed on authorial intent. Students were taught either to rank the author's intent first in interpretation or to ignore it altogether as unnecessary. As a teacher who has led students through a poem or story, I regularly hear them ask, with eyes narrowed, "Do you think the author meant that?" They are skeptical about the author's intention or ability. Surely the author was not considering Greek mythology when writing this Southern short story? We misunderstand the artistic process. More is at work in artistic creation than the author's intention, but these external factors do not negate the author's agency. Rather, when we interpret, we must take into account all three aspects of the reading experience: the author, their text or creation, and the reader or receiver.

In his book *Art and Faith*, Makoto Fujimura tells the story of how he began a particular painting with the intention to "capture the New Creation,"[3] but the finished art came to reveal more about eternity than he could have intended prior to making the artwork. Fujimura limited his materials to only one—oyster shells pulverized into a powder, mixed with glue. This technique is called *gofun*: through layering the white paint, which catches the light in various ways, the artist creates a spectrum of colors on the canvas. He titled the painting, before it was completed, *Sea Beyond*. While Fujimura intended to represent something theological in the painting, he discovered a more personal meaning to what the painting depicted when his mother suddenly passed away. Following her death, Fujimura stood on the beach in Los Gatos, California, and reflected on his painting, asking himself, "What is beyond the horizon?" The question became not spiritual for him but literal. A quick Google search revealed that Kamakura, Japan, lay directly beyond—a place where his mother took him as a child. "It became clear to me then," Fujimura writes, "my intuition was way ahead of me. I had been painting an elegy to my mother even before she had passed."[4] Although as an artist he had not been fully cognizant of his intuition, Fujimura recognizes that his painting revealed to him how God was at work.

Everything Is a Trinity

In every experience of reading a text, there are three elements: the author, the reader, and the text. You can remember this triad as ART—the ART of reading depends on the author, reader, and text. Imagine the three as the points of an equilateral triangle. This is the image described by Aristotle in *Rhetoric* (350 BC). While Aristotle discusses this triad in terms of speech-making, his analysis of rhetoric helps readers understand their relationship to texts of all sorts, including imaginative literature. Aristotle lines up the parts of a rhetorical situation with appeals that the speaker may rely on for persuasion: ethos, dependent on the character of the speaker or author; pathos, drawing on the emotions of the audience or reader; and logos, proofs within the text itself. When we try to understand a text, we should consider it not on its own but as part of this triad of elements. Instead of leaning toward one point of the triangle unevenly, if we keep these points in perpetual tension, we will experience a more balanced interpretation of the text, interact with the author's intention, and reflect on our emotional responses.

In *The Mind of the Maker*, Dorothy L. Sayers unintentionally baptizes Aristotle's rhetorical situation as trinitarian, though she is writing on the creator's experience more than the reader's. Quoting from her own play *The Zeal of Thy House*, Sayers explains, via a speech by St. Michael, how "every work of creation is threefold, an earthly trinity to match the heavenly." The Father begets his image in the Creative Idea; the Son, in the Creative Energy; and the Spirit, in the Creative Power. In the first stage, the creator beholds "the whole work complete at once." Then the Incarnate One, through his sweat and effort, moves the idea into matter. Finally, the Spirit endues the work with meaning "and its response in the lively soul."[5] This trinity of creation aligns as well with the reception of the work: the idea is the author's intention; the creation itself in matter is the text or logos; and the response occurs within the reader. Just as in every creation so too in every reading experience is the Trinity in action.

From ART to Art: Authorial Intent

In every experience of reading the Bible, we should imagine this capitalized, authoritative Author, Reader, Text at play within us, preparing us to interact with other nonauthorized texts. For instance, God is the Author of the Bible. As one of my students has called it, the Bible is God's collected works. There are human authors in this bibliography, but we recognize and search for the divine author who guides the story from Genesis to Revelation. If the interpreter (reader) seeks the divine author's meaning, that meaning may supersede the human author's understanding of the text at the time it was written.

So, too, an author of nonsacred literature may create something that speaks truthfully into a time different from the one in which they lived. Flannery O'Connor describes this kind of writer as a prophet, "a realist of distances,"[6] who can write further than she can see. Such vision is granted "from the standpoint of Christian orthodoxy."[7] We describe books that tap into this divine authorial intent as "timeless" or "universal," and their writers often constitute our canon: Confucius, Dante, Shakespeare, Jane Austen, or Martin Luther King Jr. We do not read the literature only as it pertains to its time period or to the author's context, though understanding those realities might help us unpack certain meaning. Just as it is helpful to know Paul was in prison when he penned 1 Timothy, it might enlighten our reading of Toni Morrison to know she was a Catholic African American writing mostly in the twentieth century.

While we may be able to garner prophetic truth from non-Christian writers, we should consider their stance toward faith when we interpret their work. Let me emphasize "when we *interpret* their work," not when we initially read. To reiterate what I've said a few times now, we need to put aside preconceptions and first enjoy the book before us. However, the secondary step is interpretation, thinking through the meaning. After reading a book, we can investigate the author and his or her intentions, theological background, and other external factors.

Pagan writers, such as Homer, were revered by the early saints such as St. Basil the Great, among others. Homer may indicate some truth about God's interaction with his creatures through the poet's depiction of the gods' intercession in mortals' lives, but his Greek and pagan culture limits how much he can reveal about this relationship. Louis Markos clarifies a distinction between the partial truth that the ancient writers foretasted and the complete truth found in Christianity: "The Christian need not reject the poetry of Homer, the teachings of Plato, or the myths of the pagans as one-hundred percent false . . . but may affirm those moments when Plato and Homer leap past their human limitations and catch a glimpse of the true glory of the triune God."[8] Through pagan authors and their literature, the Holy Spirit may author a revelation of truth.

In anti-Christian, agnostic, or atheist writers, such shadows of truth, when they present themselves, may still be gleaned in spite of the writers' intentions. For instance, Nietzsche meant to write against Christianity as the religion of sheep, but through his opposition, Nietzsche highlights the necessity of the faithful to relinquish power. Similarly, Zora Neale Hurston tried to write *Moses, Man of the Mountain* as a triumph of the human being named Moses, but she ultimately shows how powerless and unsuccessful such a character is without divine initiative and intervention. Following Ivan Karamazov's recitation of his diatribe against God, which is referred to as "The Grand Inquisitor," Alyosha Karamazov says, "Your poem praises Jesus, it doesn't revile him . . . as you meant it to."[9] These writers (including Ivan as the author of "The Grand Inquisitor") were often raised in churches or church-haunted cultures, and thus they exhibit remnants of faith left over in their writing. Some secular authors of the twenty-first century, however, possess none of the same vocabulary or images; they do not share the same cultural reservoir as the church. Even so, any inklings of faith in these non-Christian writers possess the potential to be baptized by a believer's interpretation.

From ART to Art: Logos and Text

In the imagination of the early church, encountering the Scriptures was equivalent to meeting the real presence of Jesus Christ, the Logos. Hans Boersma defines a "sacramental hermeneutic" as one that alludes "to the recognition of the real presence of the new Christ-reality hidden within the outward sacrament of the biblical text."[10] Boersma resuscitates this way of reading Scripture as good for the believer. Although John J. O'Keefe and R. R. Reno hesitate to adopt the premodern methods of the early church for interpreting Scripture, they observe how "Jesus Christ is the *hypothesis*. He reveals the logic and architecture by which a total reading of that great diversity and literal reality may be confidently pursued."[11] For the early church theologians, one met Christ in his Logos. What does this mean for literature?

When we read a book, are we having a divine encounter? No and yes. Maria Skobtsova, a Russian immigrant to Paris who died at Ravensbrück concentration camp in 1945, sought to see the image of Christ incarnate in every person she encountered. She writes, "If someone turns with his spiritual world toward the spiritual world of another person, he encounters an awesome and inspiring mystery. . . . He comes into contact with the true image of God in man, with the very icon of God incarnate in the world, with a reflection of the mystery of God's incarnation and divine manhood." In a way similar to seeking the image of God within our neighbor, we may read a book as though encountering the mystery of God. Skobtsova recognizes that the image is fallen, "veiled, distorted, and disfigured by the power of evil," but it is still there.[12] So we practice love for the text, looking for what is good and seeing redemption needed in what is not.

To read for the presence of Christ in a book is also to have your eyes and ears ready to find him when he appears. Dante's *Paradiso* opens with a praise of the "One who moves all things / permeates the universe and glows / in one part more and in another less."[13] While some books might glow more brightly with the signals to Christ—such as Evelyn Waugh's *Brideshead Revisited* or Sigrid Undset's *Kristin Lavransdatter*—other books still show signs of his reality that, in the words of O'Connor, "haunt" the text.[14] We must be looking, listening, and waiting for where Christ's reality appears in the text.

From ART to Art: The Reader

We have already discussed the way the reader must be humble, charitable, and generous in approaching a book. When reading the Bible, the Reader who fully understands the Author's meaning, as well as the Text himself, is the Holy Spirit within us. Even when reading books other than the Bible, this same Spirit aids us in becoming more like the Author and the Logos in our reading practices. The practice of reading Scripture develops within us the ART for encountering other authors and texts, and reciprocally, the hard work of reading other authors and texts builds our spiritual muscles for comprehending Scripture.

Reading as Perichoresis

In discussing the three entities of the reading experience, I am employing the language of "tension" and "work." However, I want to conclude by echoing what Alan Jacobs discusses in *A Theology of Reading: The Hermeneutics of Love*: "The best Christian theology has always understood love to be the fullest liberation and has found love best exemplified in play."[15] The act of reading should be enjoyable, and we do not want to steal all the fun out of the game by pulling back the curtain and baring the gears. This exploration of what constitutes reading should be more akin to opening the wardrobe door and finding a whole world alive just behind the surface of the ordinary. Jacobs notes that "the doctrine of the living interrelations of the persons of the Trinity" is the Greek word *perichoresis*, meaning "to dance around."[16] Our consideration of the author, investigation of the text itself, and reflection on our own reading experience should all three play together in illuminating the meaning of what we read. The purpose of highlighting how to read should be to learn the steps of the dance, that we may be free to enjoy our reading. After all, at its best, reading is an invitation to play.

BOOKMARK 3

•————•

Reading like Frederick Douglass

For centuries, the ability to read was a sign of status. Not only an external sign like a fancy dress or large house, but rather, the ability to read meant one held power. You could express your thoughts, know the tradition, stay abreast of contemporary issues, and so forth. You had influence. In contrast, the oppressed were not merely kept from wealth; they were barred from reading. Thus they were unable to protest their situation, see outside of their experience of the world, and realize the liberty of their own minds. Reading empowers people to think, to change their situation and that of others, and to not be manipulated by those who seek to control them.

Frederick Douglass

Consider the story of Frederick Douglass, born Frederick Bailey, a slave in 1818 in Maryland, later to become one of the foremost abolitionists and international orators of his time. In all three of his autobiographies, Douglass indicates learning to read as a primary turning point in his life, from being enslaved to being liberated spiritually, even prior to escaping his physical condition of slavery. Through Douglass's story, we receive a caution against the nonreading life: If reading makes one unfit to be a slave, does choosing not to read submit one to an enslaved life?

When one of Douglass's masters, Sophia Auld, began to teach the ten-year-old Douglass to read, her husband quickly intervened. "Learning would spoil the best [slave] in the world," Hugh Auld exclaimed. "If you teach that [slave] . . . how to read the Bible, there will be no keeping him. . . . It would forever unfit him for the duties of the slave." Listening to this speech, Douglass realized that reading was the path to freedom. He reflects on this encounter: Auld's "discourse was the first decidedly antislavery lecture to which it had been my lot to listen."[1] Although Auld intended to dissuade his wife from teaching Douglass to read, his words "awakened" Douglass to the key out of slavery. Douglass recalls that he assented to Auld's proposition—"Knowledge unfits a child to be a slave."[2] From then on, Douglass pursued learning how to read with passionate dedication.

Reading for Power

With fifty cents of his own money, Douglass purchased a second-hand copy of *The Columbian Orator*, which contained speeches by Cato and Cicero, dialogues of Socrates, poems by Milton, and so forth. As his biographer David Blight notes, from this reading, Douglass "garnered and cherished a vocabulary of liberation."[3] Douglass drew from his reading parallels between his own situation and that of the oppressed in the play *Slaves in Barbary*. Through reading Joseph Addison's *Cato*, Douglass learned how to link America to Rome. Addison portrays a Roman Caesar as a stand-in for the British Caesar. These selections in *The Columbian Orator* taught Douglass how to read figuratively and how to conceive of tropological and moral applications from the stories of classical heroes.

Douglass read *The Columbian Orator* repeatedly, memorizing the lessons of rhetoric and discovering how to express what was inside him. He enlarged his interior world and was able to bring it to bear on his external reality. Reading the speeches from *The Columbian Orator* aloud in the attic in solitude, Douglass realized, "The more I read them, the better I understood them; these speeches added much to my limited stock of language, and enabled me to give tongue to many interesting thoughts, which had frequently flashed through my soul, and died away for want of utterance."[4] Reading empowered Douglass, granting him not only the ability to communicate with others but also the ability to express his own thoughts and feelings. In a world that defined him as chattel, Douglass demonstrated to his oppressors that he was always human, and thus was meant to be free.

Douglass dedicated the gift of his literacy to empowering those around him. He taught others how to read, creating a Sabbath literacy school with fellow slaves. He quoted *Hamlet* and the Declaration of Independence and Scripture to call his brothers to escape their unjust lot. Douglass crafts his autobiographical narrative with the rhetorical brilliance of Augustine in his *Confessions*, leading people to experience his plight with him, empathize with the victim, and be stirred to action against the evil of slavery.

Writing for Readers

From *The Columbian Orator*, Douglass learned the aims of literature: to delight and instruct. On the art of oratory, the editor of *The Columbian Orator*, Caleb Bingham, wrote, "To instruct, to persuade, to please; these are its objects. To scatter the clouds of ignorance and error from the atmosphere of reason; to remove the film of prejudice from the mental eye; and thus to irradiate the benighted mind with the cheering beams of truth."[5] Douglass saw how literature could be a call to action—it could be read for pleasure and it could teach what was good. In *The Ebony Column*, Eric Ashley Hairston notes that *The Columbian Orator* showed Douglass how to "fuse classical lessons and *virtus* and Christian liberation and virtue."[6] These lessons became, in Douglass's rhetoric, persuasive models to end slavery in America.

Douglass imitates the classical and biblical masters. In his autobiography, he delivers a strong ethos, cultivates pathos in his readers, and substantiates his claims against slavery (logos) with evidence from his life story. He asks questions that draw in his readers: "Why am I a slave?" or, "Why are some people slaves and others masters?"[7] He teaches readers how to read his story, as Blight notes: "We are lead as his readers on the journey of an evolving, brilliant mind's bitter questioning of all around him."[8] Although Douglass tells his own life story, he does not do so from a motivation to express himself. There is no twenty-first-century selfish ambition or writing only for the writer. Instead, Douglass, from his reading, ascertains how to become a rhetorical storyteller—how to read his own life story and share it persuasively.

Hope Rooted in Tradition

For Douglass, reading contemporary literature was not enough to free his mind. Rather, by engaging the tradition, Douglass received a training in how to change the future for himself and his fellow African Americans. Without an imagination for how the world might be different than it currently is, hope is impossible; change is impossible. Such visions of the future are often ennobled by promises from the past: God's covenant with the Israelites produced the virtue of hope for a future Messiah; the world of ancient Greece and Rome served as a model for the Founding Fathers to construct a future nation; the Constitution and Declaration of Independence, not to mention the Bible and ancient writers, cultivated in Douglass a hope for a better America than the one he experienced. As Douglass "employed the Declaration of Independence, the Constitution, and the new creeds of the nation's second founding against his own country," Blight writes, "he never gave up on the Exodus story nor the majesty of Isaiah's wisdom nor Jeremiah's warnings."[9] The great tradition of the Bible, the classical authors, and the American founding documents planted in Douglass an imagination for a freer America.

We rarely imagine Douglass as an opponent of German biblical criticism, but he pushed against its influence. When his lover Ottilie Assing compelled him to read Ludwig Feuerbach, the atheist theologian who hailed from the University of Heidelberg, Douglass was unimpressed. Feuerbach sums up his argument in his lectures on religion as follows: "God did not, as the Bible says, make man in His image; on the contrary man, as I have shown in *The Essence of Christianity*, made God in his image."[10] As a discerning reader, Douglass saw through Feuerbach's tautology. He had read Scripture with a healthy skepticism, and it had taught him much about human nature and God's justice, concepts that he drew on in his autobiographies and speeches. Blight writes, "Douglass knew he never invented Isaiah. If pressed, he might have admitted that it was the other way around."[11]

Although Douglass criticized the Bible and especially the way nineteenth-century American Christians practiced their faith, he did so without throwing out Scripture and the church. Douglass insists, "What I have said respecting and against religion, I mean strictly to apply to the *slaveholding religion* of this land, with no possible reference to Christianity proper. . . . To be the friend of the one, is of necessity to be the enemy of the other. I love the pure, peaceable, and impartial Christianity of Christ: I therefore hate the corrupt, slaveholding . . . hypocritical Christianity of this land."[12] Douglass sifts the good from the bad in how he reads, in this case, the church. Similarly, Douglass reads the founding documents and other literature with an eye that refuses to castigate monolithically.

Although famous for his indicting speech "What to a Slave Is the Fourth of July?" Douglass did not discard the Constitution. In a review of Blight's biography of Douglass, Adam Gopnik writes of Douglass's insightful reading of the Constitution: "No one was ever a more critical reader of the Constitution, or, in the end, a more compelling advocate of its virtues." Gopnik highlights Douglass's conviction that criticism and advocacy need not be diametrically opposed. Rather, as much as Douglass accuses the Founders for not upholding their Christian virtues or political ideals, he argues, in Gopnik's paraphrase, that "the Constitution is solid, all that needs fixing is our way of reading it." This healthy skepticism as well as receptivity makes Douglass, in Gopnik's words, "one of the most radical *readers* of the American nineteenth century," and a model for other readers to follow.[13]

Douglass reads with the lenses of the tradition, which is why he looks forward in hope. In an 1880s speech, Douglass advises, "It is not well to forget the past. . . . Memory was given to man for some wise purpose. The past . . . is the mirror in which we may discern the dim outlines of the future and by which we may make them more symmetrical."[14] By looking into our past, by reading the great works of antiquity, including, for Douglass, the Bible, we find a way to understand our own story. Douglass wrote his three autobiographies as an effort to participate in this tradition. His work is saturated with biblical quotes, classical allusions, as well as slave songs and contemporary texts. He knew the tradition to be alive, and thus one in which he was called to participate and to pass forward.

Douglass's name reflects the vitality of the tradition in its influence on the past and potential for future change. Frederick adopted the name "Douglass" from a character in Sir Walter Scott's *Lady of the Lake*. As a fugitive, Douglass would not keep the enslaved name "Bailey." Instead, his chosen literary identity indicates how much he credited reading for his initial freedom. The move from Bailey to Douglass indicated "a new man," he writes in a letter to his former master. "Freedom has given me a new life." Instead of cowing before the white man as he was forced to do as Bailey, as a free man Douglass asserts, "If I should meet you now . . . I might summon sufficient fortitude to look you full in the face; and were you to attempt to make a slave of me, it is possible you might find me as disagreeable a subject as was the [Black Douglass of old Scotland] to whom I have just referred."[15] Douglass draws on the literary and historical character of *Black* Douglass—that is, Good Sir James Douglas, Robert the Bruce's leading commander in the fourteenth-century campaign for Scottish freedom against English rule. By assuming this new identity from a fourteenth-century literary character, Douglass embodies a new Douglass, a freedom fighter for his time and place.

Reading as Liberation

When I was discussing with another writer my book on reading for the life of the church, she protested that my topic seemed "really white." I asked her to explain. This was 2020. All around us were Black Lives Matter protests; I did not want to be writing a "white" book. From her perspective, reading was a luxury enjoyed by white, suburban housewives, whereas change was needed in the culture. We needed to be actively fighting unjust systems, not contemplating the good life from the comfort of our couches. I countered: Where would we be if Frederick Douglass, James Baldwin, Lucille Clifton, Toni Morrison, and many others had thought reading was an unnecessary luxury? Or that the contemplative life was separate from the active life? How would we know how to change the world without the vision of the good life to which we aspire? W. E. B. Du Bois may have responded to this writer, "Is this the life you grudge us, O knightly America?" Du Bois writes this question as a conclusion to his essay on the training of Black men, who deserve the "unknown treasures of their inner life" that come from reading.[16]

Black writers in America for over a century turned to the great tradition, as Douglass did, for a path to freedom. Picking up the mantle from Douglass, Anna Julia Cooper defended classical education for the Black students whom she taught in St. Louis, Missouri, at the end of the nineteenth century. She argued that reading extends one's horizon. Speaking specifically of women and defending their right to education, Cooper writes, "Her sympathies are broadened and opened and multiplied. . . . She may gather the best the world has known. She can commune with Socrates about the *daimon* he knew and to which she too can bear witness; she can revel in the majesty of Dante, the sweetness of Virgil, the simplicity of Homer, and strength of Milton. . . . Here, at last, can be communion without suspicion; friendship without misunderstanding; love without jealousy."[17] As a principal for an all-Black school, Cooper encouraged her students to read, to contemplate, to gain the freedom that comes from a thick soul. Against naysayers such as Booker T. Washington, who advocated mere vocational training for Black students, Cooper argues that we are more than producers and consumers. Whatever education is good for the best among us should be granted to all of us. Not only did Cooper go on to be the fourth African American woman to receive a PhD (at the Sorbonne, no less), many of her students continued their studies and received Ivy League educations.

Twentieth-century writers continued to draw on the reading life as the path to liberation. James Baldwin, born in Harlem to parents who had migrated north to protect their family from the racism and violence of the South, claims that he "read [himself] out of Harlem": "There were two libraries in Harlem, and by the time I was thirteen I had read every book in both libraries and I had a card downtown for Forty-Second Street. . . . What I had to do then was bring the two things together: the possibilities the books suggested and the impossibilities of the life around me."[18] In contrast to the contemporary lens being offered to him by the world, literature from the past augmented Baldwin's sight, granting him a vision of the way the world could be better. More than a clearer view of reality, literature showed Baldwin that he was not alone. He writes, "You read something that you thought only happened to you, and you discover that it happened a hundred years ago to Dostoyevsky. This is a very great liberation for the suffering, struggling person, who always thinks that he is alone."[19] In the same way that Cooper found company among Socrates and Milton, and that Du Bois famously crossed the "color line" to sit with Shakespeare and Balzac, Baldwin found friends in Dostoevsky and Dickens and others. The vision from the past of a better future, combined with a company of like-minded souls, encouraged readers such as Douglass, Cooper, and Baldwin to improve their world.

Such literature continues to compel people to active engagement. Talking to a friend about Ernest Gaines's novel *A Lesson before Dying*, I discovered that this friend had petitioned a governor to appeal a falsely convicted man and restore his record. Reading that novel had also inspired him to start a prison ministry, where he regularly teaches inmates Shakespeare, among other great authors. The reading life is not separate from the active one. Great books should light a fire within the reader's soul to be more like the heroes and saints within those pages. If we read well, reading may be as much a liberation for us and others as it was for Douglass. It is at the peril of our future that we ignore the books of the past and the voices of the dead.

Enslaved to Screens

"I can't bear television sets," James Baldwin admitted. "But I can afford not to bear them because I read books."[20] Since the end of the twentieth century and the start of the twenty-first century, the greatest hindrance to a reading life has been screens. In the 1996 children's book *Aunt Chip and the Triple Creek Dam*

Affair, a town succumbs to the allure of the television to the detriment of everyone. They use books as doorstops, ladders, and even a dam for the local creek, but no one reads anymore. Television even teaches the children at school; the screen has taken over education. We might see this parable as a warning against obsessive iPhone use, social media consumption, and streaming of content. There are so many complaints against how this technology has caused tribalism, has increased ignorance and conspiracy theories, and may be threatening democracy.

Dystopic novels prophesy that a world without readers is one where the privileged few control unthinking masses. Whether it's *1984* or *The Giver*, a repeated theme is the loss of reading, for you can better manipulate people who do not read than those who do. Who can forget the image of the books burning in *Fahrenheit 451*, Ray Bradbury's 1953 novel that recalls images of Nazis cheering on a bonfire of the classics? In Bradbury's novel, the firemen are those who start fires, specifically to burn books, versus those who put them out. People are saturated by technology, interacting with reality television through giant walls in their homes, and even sleeping with "seashells" in their ears for constant noise. But one fireman, Montag, meets a former literature professor, Faber, who lost his job years prior when the liberal arts colleges closed. He reminds Montag that "the firemen are rarely necessary. The public itself stopped reading of its own accord."[21] When the story was adapted to film in 2018, the producers altered the story line in a revelatory way. In that world, the books were all still available; they had not all been burned. Rather, to keep books from relaying complex ideas, the words had been converted into ideograms. Is this the way the world ends? Not with a bonfire but with an emoji?

Years ago, while attempting to invigorate first-year college students' conviction of the necessity of reading, I assigned George Orwell's "Politics and the English Language." I remember shouting, standing on a chair, waving the essay in my hand: "Do you not realize that if you do not read, you will be controlled by others?!" In *Fahrenheit 451*, the head of the fire department, Captain Beatty, recommends to Montag, "Cram them full of noncombustible data, chock them so damned full of 'facts' they feel stuffed, but absolutely 'brilliant' with information. Then they'll feel they're thinking, they'll get a sense of motion without moving. And they'll be happy, because facts of that sort don't change."[22] The captain knows how to delude people so that they are controllable. If we give them Google, they feel intelligent. If we offer them degrees where all they have to do is check boxes and answer multiple-choice quizzes, they will feel accomplished. But never lead them to love wisdom or consider their role in society. Never let them read books that encourage real thinking.

We may worry that we are steadily fulfilling Bradbury's and Orwell's prophetic imaginings of dystopia. After all, the average American today reads fewer than twenty minutes each day, in comparison to hours streaming, working, scanning social media, or just being entertained by their phones, computers, and televisions.[23] Americans are being formed more into the image of Montag's wife Mildred, who calls her virtual television cast her family and ignores her husband. At night she lies "uncovered and cold, like a body displayed on the lid of a tomb [with] her eyes fixed to the ceiling by invisible threads of steel [and] thimble radios" in her ears.[24] Such a life seems like no life at all.

However, we cannot merely turn off our screens if we do not replace them with something else. Jesus warns,

When an impure spirit comes out of a person, it goes through arid places seeking rest and does not find it. Then it says, "I will return to the house I left." When it arrives, it finds the house unoccupied, swept clean and put in order. Then it goes and takes with it seven other spirits more wicked than itself, and they go in and live there. And the final condition of that person is worse than the first. That is how it will be with this wicked generation. (Matt. 12:43–45)

Our hearts and minds will suffer greater persecution and desire for distraction if we do not fill the void with love for what is better. We may be surprised that—among other good replacements of screen time, such as walking outside, playing with children, gardening, and so forth—reading becomes not a mere substitute pastime but a spiritual practice we crave. If we are to overcome the control of media, advertising, fear tactics, and contemporary problems that loom overly large, we need a flourishing reading life. In the Word is freedom.

6

Why Do You Need
Four Senses to Read?

eading is about more than words. It is about how you *see* and *hear*. How you read written texts affects how you read the world, what the medieval writers called "the book of nature." And vice versa. "The metaphor that Christ is the 'light of the world' changes not merely the way in which we are to understand Christ, but also the way we understand *light*," observes one of my former teachers.[1] The imagination with which you read the world affects what you can comprehend in a text. Over and over again in the biblical story, the prophets warn God's chosen people that they have ears but do not hear and eyes but do not see. In the New Testament, Jesus explains how to have what Eugene Peterson translates as "God-blessed eyes—eyes that see! And God-blessed ears—ears that hear!" (Matt. 13:16 MSG). After telling a story to his disciples, he asks, "Are you listening to this? Really listening?" (13:9 MSG). Rather than leave the disciples in a state of perplexity, he unpacks the story for them, teaching them how to *read* so that they know how to really see and hear.

In church tradition, this was called "contemplation." We may assume contemplation is an isolated activity, one that leads people away from action into inner solitude. Perhaps we imagine the contemplatives from Dante's seventh heaven floating ethereally through paradise. But Peterson defines contemplation as a way of being Christian seers. He writes, "Contemplation means submitting to the biblical revelation, taking it within ourselves, and then living it unpretentiously, without fanfare. . . . Contemplation means living what we read, not wasting any of it or hoarding any of it but using it up in living."[2] After we read the Scriptures, we see everything through its lens—other books, other people, ourselves, and especially God. We become beholders, those who contemplate what they see. Through the eyes of the Word, we read everything else.

Jesus's Example of Reading

When the disciples ask Jesus why he speaks in parables, he explains the necessity of storytelling to convert people toward a higher way of seeing. Again, to borrow from Peterson's translation: "That's why I tell stories," Jesus says, "to create readiness, to nudge the people toward a welcome awakening. In their present state they can stare till doomsday and not see it, listen till they're blue in the face and not get it" (Matt. 13:11–15 MSG). Looking and listening are not sufficient; we have to receive God-blessed vision, what the church traditionally has called "contemplation." This way of seeing must be moved toward and cultivated by practice.

The parable of the sower is unique in the Gospels for being not only a parable with an attached explanation but also "a parable about parables."[3] Through the medium of the story, Jesus is explaining the necessity of story for understanding things that are hidden or transcendent. In the crowd are Pharisees who have recently upbraided Jesus because his disciples picked grain on the Sabbath. Jesus responds with one of his many "Haven't you read . . ." statements: "Haven't you read what David did when he and his companions were hungry? He entered the house of God, and he and his companions ate the consecrated bread— which was not lawful for them to do" (Matt. 12:3–4). Jesus does not dispute the legality of the action, but he submits that a story better explicates the law by showcasing its spirit and intent. Because the Pharisees read the law apart from the storied life, they legislate the law apart from the spirit.

When Jesus explains his parable, he demonstrates to his disciples how to read rightly so as not to fall into the same error as the wayward Pharisees. First, notice that Jesus references the Old Testament: he draws from Isaiah, explaining that the prophecy of deafness and blindness has been fulfilled in the Pharisees. Then Jesus unpacks the parable allegorically so the disciples can better meditate on the spiritual import. After this explication, Jesus asks whether his disciples comprehend the meaning. Because they answer yes, Jesus charges each one to act as a scribe "who brings out of his treasure what is new and what is old," a tropological act (Matt. 13:52 NRSV). Last, we should notice the eschatological sense of the story that Jesus indicates with reference to "the end of the age" (13:39 NRSV). Ultimately, the significance of the parable extends beyond the ethical: understanding the story is a matter of eternal life or death.

Four Senses and Four Rungs

Jesus illustrates four practices of reading that correspond to the four senses of meaning in Scripture. The early church exegetes practiced reading according to these four senses: the literal, figurative, moral, and anagogical meanings of the text. The senses matter because every element of creation possesses at least a twofold significance: word and meaning, law and spirit, body and soul. Without recognizing the complexity of existence, we reduce our vision. We limit our way of seeing to only what is on the surface or in the present or immediately useful. David Lyle Jeffrey explains that the four senses are "Scripture's way of mediating what happened once in time to all times and all places spiritually, and it is the Church reading Scripture attentively together, against and across time, which keeps the errata of any given moment—its politics and fallen, self-justifying motives—from eclipsing the authority of the Truth for all time."[4] If we are to have contemplative vision, we should practice ways of reading that take into account the four senses within a text.

The fourfold method was largely discarded by the Reformation, for a few reasons, which we'll later consider. Around the mid-twentieth century, however, Catholic theologians—particularly Henri de Lubac in *Medieval Exegesis*—revitalized medieval ways of reading. Here's an example from the *Collationes* of John Cassian (ca. 360–435) in which he shows how "Jerusalem can be understood in a fourfold way":

> According to history, it is the city of the Jews; according to allegory it is the Church of Christ; according to anagogy it is the city of God in heaven, which is the mother of us all; according to tropology it is the soul of man which, by this name, is frequently reviled or praised by God.[5]

These are not layered readings experienced one at a time in a specific order; rather, all four ways of perceiving the meaning of Jerusalem are always within it. When we read, we consider all four senses of its reality.

However, to arrive at a place of contemplation requires that one practice ways of reading that also align well with the senses of a text. You cannot simply become a contemplative without doing some work. A twelfth-century Carthusian monk named Guigo II (his name literally means "Guy #2") imagines contemplation as the top rung of a ladder with three preceding rungs: *lectio*, the reading of the Word; then *meditatio*, the interpretation of the meaning; and *oratio*, prayer. By these three steps we ascend toward *contemplation*. Guigo's ladder[6] is drawn from Jacob's vision in Genesis 28:10–17. Jacob dreams about a ladder established on earth, with the top reaching to heaven. "And behold," the text demands, "the angels of God ascending and descending."[7] Notice that the angels move up and down the ladder, for readers do not climb the rungs of Guigo's ladder to contemplation and remain up there. Rather, the movement toward contemplation—while we remain on earth—requires continuous ascent and descent. We read, meditate, pray, contemplate, and start over again. The practices of reading that Guigo outlines correspond with the four senses of Scripture and help us understand how to move toward contemplative reading. ·

Lectio Requires Practice

Flannery O'Connor once quipped that it was a prevalent but incorrect assumption that anyone who could read the telephone book could read literature.[8] Similarly, Peterson writes about the offhand way we approach reading Scripture. "It is not sufficient to place a Bible in a person's hands with the command, 'Read it,'" Peterson writes. "That is quite as foolish as putting a set of car keys in an adolescent's hands, giving him a Honda, and saying, 'Drive it.' And just as dangerous."[9] Too few people can read well: we cannot accurately decipher words within contexts, follow complex sentences, or attend to the details of a passage or poem. But the path to contemplation, for the medieval church, began with reading.

For Guigo and his monks, reading, or *lectio*, applies particularly to reading the Bible. Guigo defines *lectio* as "the careful study of Scripture with the soul's attention." He explains that

105

reading *seeks*; it "concerns the surface" of things. Like a foundation, reading "comes first," Guigo notes, and "accords with the exercise of the outward" knowledge of things, the external realities.[10] It is the initial step on the ladder to contemplation. For a twelfth-century monk, reading would have been performed aloud, in a community, so that each word was heard and tasted as well as seen with the eyes. To read well at this level—whether reading the Scriptures or literature—means to attend closely to the literal sense.

Literal and *Legere*

We derive our word "literal" from the Latin word for "letter." To attend to the literal sense is to attend closely to the letters. In ancient Latin manuscripts, there were no breaks between words or sentences or paragraphs.[11] The Latin word for "reading," *legere*, means "to gather," as in pulling fruit from a vine. Imagine a page of text where all the words run together. If you are to read closely, with attention, you will be harvesting out the words from the letters before you. A contemporary of Guigo, who is a more well-known master reader and teacher, is Hugh of St. Victor. In his *Didascalicon*, his manual on the art of reading, Hugh describes reading as a physical activity, not passive, the way moderns may assume. "When Hugh reads," scholar Ivan Illich notes, "he harvests; he picks the berries from the lines."[12] A literal reading involves gathering the fruit, tasting the syllables of the text, chanting the words, and chewing on them.

In monastic culture, the monks read not only Scripture but also classical literature (both aloud) to learn it by heart. "The repeated mastication of the divine words [became] spiritual nutrition," Jean Leclercq writes. They used the language of eating and digestion because of the connotation of *ruminatio*, which means chewing and metaphorically can refer to meditation.

Leclercq describes how the oral pronunciation of the words resulted in "muscular memory of the words pronounced and an aural memory of the words heard."[13] This practice of reading aloud was also part of meditation, the second step of the ladder on the way to contemplation. It is as difficult to parse out these steps from one another as it is to fully untwine the four senses that are so intimately connected.

For twenty-first-century readers, we should imitate this lost way of reading so we might know by heart what we read. No longer do our words run together on the page as they did in Latin, but we should continue to ask, How might we attend to words as closely as they deserve? What if *lectio* began with reading aloud, with feeling the words on your tongue and teeth and practicing the sounds and noticing where they occur in your mouth and throat? When reading Scripture, we are feeding on the Word. Peterson insists that in addition to learning Scripture, we should digest the words within us: "Not merely Read your Bible but *Eat this book*."[14] Jesus Christ is called the Word, and we are to dine on his body—not only in the sacrament of Communion but also in our devotional reading. Recall George Herbert's poem "Love III," in which Love says to his guest, "You must sit down . . . and taste my meat."[15] To read literature well, we should articulate the choice words aloud, delighting in the sounds of sentences and the ways the beautiful diction tastes.

If you practice reading aloud "Easter Wings," also by George Herbert, you will notice how necessary is every choice of diction in the poem.[16] The sounds of the poem correlate with both the descending emotion and the confession of the speaker. When Herbert attempts to register the feelings of sorrow, despair, or shame, he employs the low-sounding vowels: *store, same, fool, decay, more, became, most, poor,* and so on. Consider that long *o* or *a* occurs low in your throat. I often point out to readers that you must strain to smile when pronouncing those low *o* and *a* sounds; they compel you to feel the sorrow when articulating them.

The second and fourth stanzas of "Easter Wings" change midway through to higher sounds as the speaker recalls repentance and salvation. To experience the speaker's elation, the poet increases the number of long *i*, *e*, and short *a* sounds: *rise, victories, fall, flight,* and so on. What occurs is a physical experience of the poem in its literal and spiritual meaning. These words signify meaning, and we feel their weight and height more profoundly when we orally express and audibly receive them.

Reading the Letters

The early church writers and medieval monks emphasized the knowledge of the literal sense as a precursor to figurative interpretation. Too often, contemporary readers jump past what a text actually says to what they think it means. At the same time, we hear the phrase "literal meaning" as that which excludes figurative reality. I once overheard a conversation where someone who believed that the earth was flat because of her literal interpretation of the Bible was asked, "How do you read the phrase 'God is a lion'?" I thought the question quite on point. If we read the claim "God is a lion" as literally true, we end up mocking God. Instead, if we read the phrase on the literal level as possessing a metaphor, we might spark the imagination of a C. S. Lewis to create more enduring children's stories about Aslan the lion, king of the whole wood. For the patristic writers, we should read the metaphors well by attending to the literal sense of the words themselves.

To attend to the literal sense of a passage in Scripture is time-consuming. We must consider what each word means. We examine its definition, the context of the words around it, the etymology of the word, the connotations, and the historical meaning.

To take a literary example, if we read George Herbert's poem "The Windows" where he writes of "crazy glass," we might think "crazy" means mentally unsteady.[17] However, in the seventeenth century, the word meant "broken." We have to know the words and what they mean to realize that Herbert is pointing to the stained glass in a cathedral.

When we read texts not written in English, knowing the words of the original language becomes crucial to interpretation. I remember when I first discovered that the King James Version had changed Jesus's occupation from "builder" to "carpenter."[18] The translators interpreted "builder" according to their British knowledge of a builder, which in the seventeenth century was someone who worked with wood. Yet, in first-century Palestine, Jesus as a builder would have worked with stone. He would have been more like a mason. Of course, the meaning of words is important to understand literature but paramount to interpret the Word of God. If we dedicate ourselves to clarifying the meaning of words in literature, we are more attuned to this need in our Bible reading.

For the patristic writers, who heard words read aloud, puns also became a source of perceiving the text. They would play with words that sounded like the word being used and reflect on what such a game drew out for them. That might sound dangerous. Without piety and humility, it is. But these early church thinkers believed that the God who authored creation created language, leaving all sorts of clues for interpretation within words. We can practice this playfulness by reading whimsical poems. Consider the fun of "Jabberwocky," in which many of the words have no English meaning. Yet the poem's words inspire every feeling that it intends: "'Twas brillig, and the slithy toves / Did gyre and gimble in the wabe."[19] It's difficult to type that poem because the computer wants to autocorrect the nonsense. But we are not computers! We can decipher meaning in the sounds. For over a century, people have memorized this poem and felt its adventure without ever needing to define etymologically the "gimble."

Historia as Literal Meaning

In addition to the words, the literal sense also includes what we mean when we say what *literally* happened—the action of the story. In an essay on Dante's employment of the four senses, his translator Dorothy L. Sayers explains the literal sense with the aid of Thomas Aquinas, who refers to it as the "historical" sense. Sayers explains that "historical" may refer to "something which really happened; or it may mean, in the wider sense of the Latin word *historia*, something which is narrated—a *story*, whether fact, myth, or fiction."[20] For the ancient biblical expositors, a literal reading of Scripture explored the details of history, the setting, the characters on the scene. Hugh of St. Victor advises his monks to first ground themselves well in this history: "You learn history and diligently commit to memory the truth of the deeds that have been performed, reviewing from beginning to end what has been done, when it has been done, where it has been done, and by whom it has been done."[21] For instance, Jesus was a first-century Jew in Roman-occupied Palestine. Knowing about this historical context, the ancient culture, and the Old Testament elucidates the Gospels. Similarly, in literary reading, knowing the literal sense means considering what happens in the story, as well as the cultural context, assumptions, and so forth.

When Flannery O'Connor was asked to read her short story "A Good Man Is Hard to Find," a reader raised a hand to inquire about the significance of the Misfit's hat. To which O'Connor retorted that the hat was meant to cover his head. We cannot get so caught up in the "what-is-the-significance"[22] that we neglect the literal story. O'Connor hoped we would enjoy the story for what it is without leaping too quickly to "solve" it. "Properly, you analyze to enjoy," O'Connor writes, "but it's equally true that to analyze with any discrimination, you have to have enjoyed already."[23] Stories and poems, as I've mentioned, are not problems to be solved but works to be enjoyed. This enjoyment begins by appreciating the work on its literal level.

Spiritual Reading

If the phrase "reading spiritually" conjures up a yogi with closed eyes chanting on his carpet, then we need to replace that image and any hurdles it causes for readers. Instead, imagine a mother reading aloud to her children in the living room, each child snuggled beside her, as she intones the words with her young ones, pausing intermittently to ask what they are feeling, thinking, and delighting in. Or try to go back in time and picture Julian of Norwich, in her anchoress cell attached to the cathedral, mulling over the visions that God lay before her, realizing in her heart that the meaning of the showings was love, always love, forever love. Maybe you hear monks humming like bees as they read the texts they are copying aloud and ruminating—meditating—on the words before them. Or you might see a pastor walking up and down in his office, wearing thin the beige carpet beneath his feet, asking himself questions and mumbling answers.

In *lectio divina*, reading, meditation, and prayer are united. However, to understand how to read as a spiritual exercise, we will parse out each element of the practice. Just as *lectio divina* is threefold, Sayers notes in an essay on *The Divine Comedy* that the spiritual sense of a work includes three senses—the allegorical, the tropological, and the anagogical. To pull apart the senses may feel as silly as cutting a rainbow into separate strips of light. However, by staring closely at the violet or the indigo, we can see the way the colors work with one another to create such a beautiful sight. So, too, with zooming in on the practices and senses one by one.

Scholastic versus Monastic Readers

Reading the Bible is not just for academics, pastors, or theologians, any more than reading literature is only for scholars or writers. Recently I was talking with a Christian woman who was kind enough to drive me to and from a speaking engagement; she told me that prior to my talk, she had not thought of reading the Bible. For years, she had preferred books on Christian living because she had convinced herself they were just like the Bible but more accessible. Some churches de-emphasize Bible reading and focus on topics drawn from Scripture because they assume that the study of the Word belongs to the leadership of a congregation. We misconstrue the Christian's calling in relationship to the Word and words when we think of our Bible reading only in terms of study.

In his history of the ways medieval monks read the Bible and classical literature, Jean Leclercq distinguishes studying from meditative reading. He calls the former scholastic and the second monastic:

> The scholastic *lectio* takes the direction of *quaestio* and *disputatio*. The reader puts questions to the text and then questions himself on the subject matter: *quaeri solet*. The monastic *lectio* is oriented toward the *meditatio* and the *oratio*. The objective of the first is science and knowledge; of the second, wisdom and appreciation. In the monastery, the *lectio divina*, this activity which begins with grammar, terminated in compunction, in desire of heaven.[24]

Scholastic readers, those who study the text, engage in conversation with the material, quizzing it, catechizing themselves through the reading of the book, arguing for and against its claims. Whereas the monastic reader moves toward praying the text, loving it, and digesting it.

Both scholastic and monastic ways of reading are open to all readers, but the monastic method is probably more appealing to a majority of readers, and its end is higher. In *You Are What You Love*, James K. A. Smith dismisses the scholastic reading: "Jesus is not Lecturer-in-Chief; his school of charity is not like a lecture hall where we passively take notes while Jesus spouts facts about himself in a litany of text-heavy PowerPoint slides."[25] Because the Bible consists of Jesus's words as a way of life, the monastic reader submits to the story, to being formed in a new mold by the words on which she meditates day and night. Instead of concluding with mere knowledge, which may strengthen or puff up a soul, the monastic reader lives out what she learns in wisdom and the love of God.

Associative Reading

In his commentary on Proverbs, Thomas Aquinas writes of divine wisdom "always at play, playing through the whole world."[26] Rather than being a stuffy or overly serious activity, meditation should be leisurely, playful, freeing. When Gregory the Great composed a sermon on Ezekiel, for example, he expended hundreds of words on a single verse at a time. He meditates on a line that appears to be only literal, such as "six cubits and a handbreath," and draws out the implication for the active life "signified by the six cubits and the contemplative life by the handbreadth because we complete the former by works, but even when we strive concerning the latter we hardly avail to attain too little."[27] From this meditation, which moves him toward a figurative sense of the words, Gregory gathers in the story of Mary and Martha from Luke 10:38–42 and compares the active Martha with the contemplative Mary. Then he reverts to the Old Testament again, seeing an analogy between active Leah and contemplative Rachel in Genesis. Playing with words and images in this way, Gregory moves back and forth through the whole of Scripture. Because he knows the two Testaments share one Author, Gregory can draw freely from all of God's story. And because Gregory knows his beloved book by heart, he can effortlessly associate Genesis with Ezekiel with Luke from memory.

So much can be said for these associative reading practices in literature. For instance, scholars for years have enjoyed tracing the motif of eyes in Joseph Conrad's novels or the meaning of Blackness in Alice Walker's stories. Yet many readers associate words or images across their reading without a scholarly purpose. How fun and freeing it is to trace words across the tradition and see what truths or contentions arise! John O'Keefe and R. R. Reno call this practice "associative reading," in which "specific words and images function more like intersections of forces than placeholders for determinate and fixed meanings."[28] Postmodern critics relish this deconstructing of words, but that's not what the patristic and monastic writers were after. They believed that the play between words was meaningful, for God spoke creation into existence with words, Christ calls himself the Word, and God's laws are called his Ten Words, thus all this knowledge points to words being saturated with spiritual potency.

In a similar manner to how Gregory the Great and other early church writers associated words across the Scriptures, readers can understand a text better by meditating on the figurative connotations, intertextual relations, and mythic sources of words. For example, take the word "fire" in Cormac McCarthy's novel *The Road*.[29] Each day that they can, the father and the boy build a fire for heat, to dry them, to cook with. They build a fire, stoke the fire, rekindle the fire. In one sense, the daily building of the fire is a beautiful reminder of the necessity of the small tasks that constitute a life. But the fire also figures allegorically. The fire within the boy is that fire of love that created us, as Catherine of Siena puts it.[30] It is the fire of knowledge as a gift of the gods. It is the fire that "came from the holy flame," as Statius says of the *Aeneid*,[31] the fire of the tradition itself handed down and embodied by those who live it. The father and son are the "good guys" in the novel because they "carry the fire."

There is, in many ancient stories, the resonance of fire as a divine emblem. It burns upward and draws our eyes heavenward. In one of the purportedly earliest religions, Zoroastrianism, fire was revered as a purifying agent. The Greco-Roman world thought of fire as stolen from the gods for human beings—for hearth and kiln—but fire also became associated with knowledge.[32] In the Hebrew Scriptures, God speaks through a burning bush and guides the Israelites through the desert by a pillar of fire. In *The Road*, the fire in the little boy is, as the father intimates, connected to the Word of God—"If he is not the word of God God never spoke."[33]

To read the fire in this way keeps the tradition of spiritual reading alive; we are asked by the narrative to read patterns within the text, within the world, across time and place. Patterns are what grant meaning to a work of art. The image of carrying the fire, as it is repeated throughout *The Road*, gains significance and becomes a thicker and fuller image in our experience of the story. Now, none of these examples from antiquity are in *The Road*, but those with a collective cultural memory read fire in light of its associations across the tradition.

When Sayers writes on language, she justifies associative reading: "Every word is an *event*. . . . Poetic language is a web of light, the whole of which is spread through time and space, and quivers at every touch."[34] Words invite us to consider their previous uses, contexts, and worlds. We gain a fuller understanding of truth, beauty, and goodness from meditating on a word's pattern found throughout literature, history, and tradition.

Meditation and Allegory in Scripture

Unfortunately, such playfulness with a text as authoritative as Scripture has been denounced for half a millennium, starting with Martin Luther and his rants against allegory. For Luther and like-minded Reformers, the concern was the hazard of unsound doctrine, allegory composed by irreverent meditation. Luther insists, "It is dangerous to play with the word of God. . . . The natural meaning of the words is queen, transcending all subtle, acute sophistical fancy."[35] Over and against allegory, Luther prizes the literal interpretation of Scripture. He advises against playful meditation on the text, calling those who rely on these methods "spiritual jugglers." As a monk, Luther learned how to imitate St. Jerome and Origen, not to mention St. Augustine. "I was a master in the use of allegory. I allegorized everything," Luther reflects. But after he left the church, he declares, "It's not what Christ signified but what Christ is that counts."[36] As with much of Luther's writing, his style is rhetorically persuasive. Yes, we all want to nod our heads, what Christ *is* matters most.

However, "Christ" is itself a word with multiple layers of meaning. The word signifies beyond its letters. The Hebrew for Christ is *mashiach*—"Messiah"—and fulfills the prophetic imagination and allegorical meaning of much of the Old Testament. In Greek, the word *Christos* was invented from "anointed one" because they had no such need of the word "messiah" in their language. All these meditations on the meaning of Christ are necessary in knowing who Christ is, and then more to explore the significance of "Christ" in relation to the historical Jesus.

When Peterson writes on meditation, he encourages the "playful curiosity of a child" rather than the "cool and detached expertise" of a theologian. If we are to become "empathetic with the text," we must meditate on the words, considering the fullness of their meaning, getting to know the side that is not immediately apparent or forthcoming.[37] Meditating on the Bible should lead us not to selfish observations or fanciful conclusions but to becoming better friends with the presence within the book—Christ himself. "Meditation," Peterson writes, "moves from looking at the *words* of the text to entering the *world* of the text."[38] After we have dedicated time to the literal and historical reading of

116

the words, we enter into the fuller picture, the spiritual reality revealed to us through those particular words.

Allegory in Literature

The problem that faces allegorical interpretation in literature is often one of misdefining the word itself. C. S. Lewis and J. R. R. Tolkien have famously protested against the word "allegory" being applied to their stories. In the preface to his science fiction novel *Perelandra*, Lewis insists, "All the human characters in this book are purely fictions, and none of them is allegorical."[39] Likewise, Tolkien takes care to dissuade readers of *The Lord of the Rings* in his foreword to the second edition: "I cordially dislike allegory in all its manifestations, and always have done so since I grew old and wary enough to detect its presence."[40] However, they are both referring to a simplistic rendering of allegory that controls the reader's response with a one-to-one correlation between sign and symbol. Tolkien admits as much in his foreword when he writes, "I much prefer history—true or feigned—with its varied applicability to the thought and experience of readers. I think that many confuse applicability with allegory, but the one resides in the freedom of the reader, and the other in the purposed domination of the author."[41] While Tolkien tries to differentiate applicability from allegory, the distinction merely robs the word "allegory" of its more inclusive meaning.

In her attempt to revitalize the genre of allegory, Sayers uplifts *The Divine Comedy*, *The Faerie Queene*, and *The Pilgrim's Progress*, but then disregards *Perelandra* as being as unallegorical as its author claims. Regarding our misappropriation of the word "allegory," Sayers quips, "We are in the same situation as an American who, not knowing the first thing about cricket, is planked down in the pavilion at Lord's to watch a Test Match."[42] I'm grateful Sayers had the humility to include herself in the "We" of that sentence. For she adheres to the same assumptions that misled Lewis and Tolkien. She writes against the long life of "allegorical interpretation of Scripture" and is thankful for the modern biblical criticism that has replaced it. Sayers no longer suffers sermons on allegory, for "the Bible," in Sayers's reading, "though rich in myth and parable, is almost barren of allegory."[43] The German biblical critics had done their job and persuaded the masses against allegorical reading.

For all the protest against allegory, Sayers understood how to read literature allegorically, at least when it came to Dante. Even Lewis and Tolkien wrote literature that should be read for its spiritual as well as literal sense. Lewis's *Perelandra* is a retelling of the Eden story as set on the planet Venus, so we may freely meditate on connections between the characters and the Genesis story, as well as connections with other origin myths. To read the novel with its spiritual sense does not denude it of a literal plot. We need not reduce the Green Lady to Eve, but we can ruminate on how the characters highlight or contrast with one another. Or, in Tolkien's world, Aragorn is a Christ figure, but so are the hobbits and Gandalf and all who reflect the manifold nature of the incarnate God. People typically consider allegory as stories with one-to-one correlations, as we would find in Bunyan's *Pilgrim's Progress*. However, to read allegorically is to find a plethora of spiritual correlations in the text. For Lewis, Tolkien, and Sayers, their limited definition of the word "allegory" prevented them from seeing their own work as allegorical. All three authors can be read as *ressourcement* readers—like Henri de Lubac or Hans Urs von Balthasar—who return us to medieval modes of reading texts and seeing the world spiritually.

For the medieval reader, the world was "charged with the grandeur of God,"[44] so medieval writers told stories at both a literal and spiritual level. When contemporary Protestants read Dante, they struggle with how much the spiritual reality has come to the surface of that world. For instance, Dante says he finds himself lost in a wood, which is literally true and spiritually resonant of the state of his soul. He has lost his purpose as a person. Dante's state of being lost in the woods connotes the Israelites lost in the wilderness, away from God's promised land. Then Dante faces three beasts. Although the beasts are physically guarding against his climb up a mountain, they spiritually represent sins that keep Dante from ascending. The leopard signifies lust, the lion symbolizes pride, and the wolf represents greed. Medieval readers would have understood those meanings without need of an instructor, for symbology was part and parcel of how they read the world.

This medieval tradition extends backward into Jewish culture. In the Hebraic alphabet, letters hold numeric meaning, such as the *yod*, the tenth letter, which also signifies fullness, completion, the beginning of creation, the first letter of the names of Israel, Jacob, Judah, Jesus, and so forth. The word "yod" means hand, and the letter's shape looks like a person both lowering herself in prayer and pointed upward to God.[45] Because the Hebrew Bible relies on physical things for revealing God, "Hebrew mysticism is paradoxically concretely rooted in the Incarnation, of the Word as flesh and blood, with simple things we see and taste, with *mem* being water, and *nun*, fish; that God's Word . . . is in all Creation."[46] One could stare at a letter in the Hebrew Bible, meditate on its meaning, and come to know God better, what is called cataphatic mysticism. Yet the goal was not mystical reverie for the reader but praise of the Creator who signed his name in every jot and atom.

Christians in the early church retained practices of reading texts closely so they could better interpret God's spiritual movement in their physical world. In *De Doctrina Christiana*, Augustine advises readers to know about animals, plants, and numbers, to be able to understand God's figurative and mystical meanings: "Ignorance of things . . . renders figurative expressions obscure, as when we do not know the nature of the animals, or minerals, or plants, which are frequently referred to in

Scripture by way of comparison."[47] Medieval bestiaries listed the allegorical meaning of all animals. For example, of the wolf, the Aberdeen Bestiary tells us that wolves' eyes shine in the night. We can read this spiritually: "The wolf's eyes shine in the night like lamps because the works of the Devil seem beautiful and wholesome to blind and foolish men."[48] By modern criteria, we might find such symbolism far-fetched, "but for the ancients they were founded on reality," Leclercq reminds us.[49] Different animals, plants, stars, bodies of water could show characteristics of God or morals for the believer.

We're so accustomed to passive entertainment that informs us what to feel and think about a story, through camera angles, pacing, music, and so forth, that our imaginations have become rather lazy. Leclercq uplifts the monks for their engaged ways of seeing what was before them: "The sanctification of the imagination results in their attachments to the slightest particulars of the text, and not merely to the ideas it contains."[50] Rather than gaze past the words on the page, the medieval readers looked into the text to discover the spiritual sense. For centuries, Christians saw the whole world in light of what they had practiced reading within texts. We should draw from these predecessors what is worthy of imitation and reclaim these lost ways of encountering the Lord through his words and works.

When we read literature, spiritual knowledge of animals, plants, numbers can illuminate even contemporary works, for the world is enchanted by significance. We get to investigate the cultural assumptions of the author, the context of the text, and so forth. Do dragons mean the same thing in Lewis and Tolkien as they do in *Wings of Fire*? How is the lion in Dante's *Inferno* unlike the Lion of Judah? In what ways do Eastern versus Western writers read fig trees? Is the number ten always symbolic of perfection and wholeness? There is so much to see and behold that should not be taken for granted, so much from which to glean more knowledge of God. If we are seeking meaning rather than assuming meaninglessness, we will be rewarded by our rich reading practices.

Personal Relationship with the Book

In the Roman Empire, people would flip through the *Aeneid* and point their finger at a passage, then they would read it prophetically, as though the epic poem were speaking to them like a fortune cookie. When St. Augustine hears a child's voice calling, "*Tolle, lege*" (Take up and read), he treats the Bible in this same mode: he flips it open to a passage, reads it aloud, then declares the text to have spoken imperatively to him.[51] I myself recall—having no knowledge of this ancient history at the time—thumbing through my own Bible and alighting on verses as though they were intended for me in that moment. We've been enculturated to read tropologically. While that five-dollar sentence is fun, here's another way to say it: The culture has taught us to ask when we read, What does this book mean to me?

The tropological sense of the Bible is the third sense for a reason. It requires the first two senses to be attended to. In *How (Not) to Read the Bible*, Dan Kimball warns that "if we view the Bible as mainly a 'message for me,' we will be in great trouble."[52] First we need to discern the literal and historical—the original audience, the human author, and the meaning of the original language—as well as the allegorical or spiritual significance before we read the words of the Bible tropologically. Without initially examining the literal and spiritual sense, we "will end up picking and choosing the things we like reading and want to apply to our lives."[53] Our knowledge of the Bible will be composed of our favorite verses about God's blessings. We will never wrestle with or be scandalized by the awe-inspiring character of God.

After writing his manual on how to read, which primarily focuses on *historia* and *allegoria*, Hugh of St. Victor dedicates an entire book to tropological formation.[54] Reading begins the journey or ascent to virtue, but the practice of a life well lived must follow. As one scholar explains, in Hugh's imagination, the literal reading is the foundation, allegory is the edifice, and then one paints "the building's exterior with the beautiful colors of the moral life by means of *tropologia*."[55] We practice what we read, and this operation of a good life moves us toward the source of virtue, God. Hugh writes, "The discipline of God orders [the human being] into his end because, reforming the human fully and perfectly through virtue, it leads him through to beatitude."[56] The practice of virtuous living is a road to God, a rung on the ladder toward the beatific vision.

On Guigo's ladder, the third rung is *oratio*, or prayer, which is en route toward contemplation, so we should think of the tropological reading as a way station. If we treat the tropological reading as an end in itself, we risk demoting our ethical reading to "static, lifeless, moralism," as Ryan McDermott, the author of a book on tropology, points out. McDermott highlights how common the tropological reading is in our culture: "in everything from Sunday sermons and the VeggieTales to Kindle readers' private notes and YouVersion users' public commentary." Yet this way of reading should be commuting "words into the works for the love of God and neighbor and, ultimately, for the sake of salvation."[57] We should not be satisfied with improving our personal character, but we should be directed toward the One who transfigures us into his likeness.

Oratio and Moral Reading

The tropological sense may be associated with the third rung in Guigo's ladder because we are turning God's words into our prayer, converting what has been memorized in our hearts into how we see and act in the world. Hans Urs von Balthasar writes, "In the *meditatio* . . . we are invited first to imagine the scene with our 'mind,' then to grasp its content with the 'reason,' and finally to embrace with the 'will' and the 'affections' what has been understood, to appropriate it and build it into our own lives."[58] The believer may read Isaiah's prophecy regarding Christ, "he was pierced for our transgressions, / he was crushed for our iniquities" (Isa. 53:5), and understand first the literal meaning of the crucifixion, allegorically the significance of a suffering and dying God, and finally the reality of the call to suffer likewise—to take up one's cross. Through prayer, the words of Scripture become action.

Perhaps we only think of prayer as a dialogue between us and God in the quiet of our homes or around our dinner tables or as a segue between hymns at church. But prayer "is our entrance into the grammar of revelation, the grammar of the word of God."[59] Because there is so much about God that is beyond our comprehension and so much about his world and his creatures and eternity that will require a lifetime of beholding and attending, we practice prayer to ready us for more and more of him. Peterson explains, "That is why we *pray* what we read. Prayer is the way we work our way out of the comfortable but cramped world of self into the self-denying but spacious world of God."[60] To pray what we read need not be confined only to the words of Scripture; it might also be the prayers of the tradition, prayers of the people, prayers from literature.

When reading Michael O'Brien's novel *Father Elijah*, I felt compelled to pray. I had chosen the book because of its apocalyptic plot: I had planned to enjoy a fun ride through the end of the world. But I was blindsided by a moment when a Holocaust survivor confronts an unrepentant Nazi who glories in his murders. The details may be muddled in my mind, yet I remember well how the acts that should have been confessed were nearly spit from this dying man's mouth, and how the priest, a Jew, still forgave him. Lying in my warm bed, nearly nodding off to sleep, I experienced a sudden compulsion to wake up, flip off my covers, and go to my knees beside the bed. By my lamp, an icon was hanging. I began to pray and cry and pray, "Lord, let me forgive even those whom I don't want to forgive, those against whom I've held on to my resentment or justified my grievances. Lord, let me forgive like Father Elijah forgave." I asked to be as holy as the fictional character whose story I had just witnessed.

This way of praying is how we "pray without ceasing," for it becomes our habit (1 Thess. 5:17 NRSV). "Prayer by prayer, we find ourselves living in a reality that is far larger, far lovelier, far better," Peterson writes.[61] Just as our prayer life transforms our activities into acts of love, so our tropological reading transfigures the words we've loved into works of love in our lives. By this spiritual practice of reading, we embody the way of Christ.

Books to Be Prayed

In reading literature, the tropological way of reading does not mean we pray the text itself, as we would with Scripture in *lectio divina*. Though there have been many books published that collect the spiritual writings of an author into one place or are titled *The Gospel according to . . .* ,[62] we need to ask of a book, "Can you live it? Can you put it into action? Can you speak—or adapt—the language of this work, use it to talk to both yourself and others so as to live better?"[63] To read tropologically, the book becomes part of how we live and speak. If a friend is undergoing a crisis, I might cite an encouraging piece of Scripture, but I also might draw from the reservoir of beautiful passages within me from literature or the wise words of geniuses from our tradition. Only because we are out of practice does it seem pretentious in our conversations with others to offer up the best that has been thought and said.

Moreover, we should read new creations of art as tropological readings of texts. When a person reads tropologically, they create in response to what they have internalized—in how they live their life, how they pray, or what they create. McDermott offers the examples of *Piers Plowman* and other medieval pageantry plays as tropological interpretations of Scripture. George Steiner, a non-Christian critic, stood against his contemporaries the deconstructionist critics when he said that the best reading was to bring forth the presence of the past text. He calls *The Divine Comedy* the best "reading of the *Aeneid*, technically and spiritually 'at home,' 'authorized' in the several and interactive senses of that word, as no extrinsic commentary by one who is himself not a poet can be."[64] Although Steiner was not functioning under a sacramental paradigm, which assumes the power of texts to be enfleshed, his experience with literature taught him this reality.

"The best readings of art are art," Steiner contends. When we read a work so closely that it becomes part of how we see the world, then we will create under its influence. We will read all else by its light. Hence, reading Scripture should be our primary and daily reading. "Art develops via reflection and on preceding art, where 'reflection' signifies both a 'mirroring' and a 're-thinking,'" Steiner explains. "It is through this internalized 're-production' of an amendment to previous representations that an artist will articulate what might appear to have been even the most spontaneous, the most realistic of his sightings."[65] The illusion of originality may deceive us that we should abscond from all influences, but the God who made us in his image calls us, as a salvific imperative, to the *imitatio Christi*.

Contemplative Reading and the Anagogical Imagination

The end of all our reading should be contemplation. Our active life, fostered by tropological reading, will be frenetic, fruitless, and unsatisfying without contemplation, which is the way of knowing the Maker of all meaning. To be a contemplative does not mean one becomes a hermit. Rather, as Kathleen Norris indicates in *The Quotidian Mysteries*, "The true mystics of the quotidian are not like those who contemplate holiness in isolation, reaching godlike illumination in serene silence, but those who manage to find God in a life filled with noise, the demands of other people and relentless daily duties that can consume the self."[66] We become habituated to contemplating God through our daily lives by the practice of spiritual reading. Balthasar agrees: "Unavoidably, the life of contemplation is an everyday life, a life of fidelity in small matters, small services rendered in the spirit and warmth of love which lightens every burden."[67]

The way we read books will foster a certain imagination, a particular way of reading the world, in which we ascend toward contemplating God and all his graces or descend into utilitarianism and reduced vision. John Henry Newman writes, "Christ lives, to our imaginations, by His visible symbols."[68] And not only by sacraments, adds Stephen Prickett, "but by the whole complex web of visual iconography and literary metaphor which has grown from the Bible and the associated traditions of the Church."[69] If we first closely consider the letters or images of a text, the literal and historical meaning, then dig deeper to explore the allegorical or spiritual significance, we must discern not only how we shall live but also what we have discovered about the One who is our life. In Christian tradition, the anagogical sense refers to a text's echo or reflection of the divine. Where do we see God here? Or we might equate the anagogical with the eschatological: Knowing that all will end in our death and Christ's second coming, what matters in what we have read? It's the cultivation of a sight that points our eyes ever upward toward heaven.

Guigo assumes that the process of contemplation is repetitive within this life, so one is always crafting an anagogical imagination that considers the particular, the spiritual, the moral, and the final ends. These four senses are ways of reading that prepare one for a certain practice of seeing the world, of being a contemplative. Whereas the world trains us toward a utilitarian vision that is consumerist and destructive, the contemplative remains open to mystery and enchantment, beholding what is concrete, seeking the poetic. The contemplative vision is ultimately life-giving.

In his 1945 science fiction novel *That Hideous Strength*, C. S. Lewis contrasts the lack of imagination of the utilitarian to the contemplative, anagogical vision. At the start of the novel, a group of faculty gathers together at Bracton College to discuss selling off a portion of their property called the Bragdon Wood. The bursar holds up a map and identifies the task at hand as whether to sell the "area coloured pink on the plan, which, with the Warden's permission, I will now pass around the table."[70] Notice how the faculty see the land. It has been quantified by acreage, marked on a map, examined on a sheet of paper from a distance. It has no smell, no sounds, no beauty. Instead of a place with a story and a history, the faculty reduce the land to an amenity. They interpret the location by its data, utility, and resources. With this imagination toward their "resource," the faculty vote to sell the wood.

In contrast with this impersonalized vision of the Bragdon Wood, our unnamed narrator (who is, for all purposes, Lewis himself) has enjoyed a recent stroll through this particular wood. He describes a high wall enclosing it, and when you enter, you sense a "gradual penetration into a holy of holies." The narrator invites the reader to join him on this expedition, writing in the second-person *you*:

> First you went through the Newton quadrangle which is dry and gravelly; florid, but beautiful Gregorian buildings look down upon it. Next you must enter a cool tunnel-like passage, nearly dark at mid-day . . . [that bears] a whiff of the smell of fresh bread. . . . The grass here looks very green after the aridity of Newton and the very stone of the buttresses that rise from it

gives the impression of being soft and alive. Chapel is not far off: the hoarse, heavy noise of the works of a great and old clock comes to you from somewhere overhead. . . . You were in a sweet, Protestant world. You found yourself, perhaps thinking of Bunyan or of Walton's *Lives*. . . . As I went forward over the quiet turf, I had the sense of being received. The trees were just so wide apart that one saw uninterrupted foliage in the distance but the place where one stood seemed always to be a clearing; surrounded by a world of shadows, one walked in mild sunshine.[71]

The difference between these two ways of seeing should be striking. All of the senses are turned on—the smell of bread, the play of the sunlight. The literary allusions to Bunyan and Walton are called up. The hint of the possibility of a divine Host or Giver. Everything in our experience is heightened by his description, our souls evoked by its beauty. When it comes to which way we want to be in the world, the latter accords more with the Christian vision of the world.

However, a contemplative vision has to be cultivated. We do not simply exist as a faculty member examining data or as a man walking through a wood in meditation. We make small, significant choices that form the imagination to see according to one set of lenses versus another. We practice ways of reading spiritually that ascend a ladder toward contemplation. We learn the four senses and practice reading with them.

7

How Can You Remember
What You Read?

The film adaptation of *The Fellowship of the Ring* opens with the angelic but haunting voice of the Elvish Lady Galadriel cautioning listeners, "Much that once was is lost. For none now live who remember it." She relays the story of the ring of power, and then repeats her warning: "Some things that should not have been forgotten were lost."[1] Her words call to mind, for me, the episode in the Old Testament when Hilkiah the priest uncovers the lost book of God's law in the Jewish temple. Seemingly, the book was just lying around, collecting dust, until King Josiah asked his royal secretary to send funds to the priests to restore the temple. Then the book is discovered. In Eugene Peterson's translation, he adds exclamation points in Hilkiah's speech: "I've just found the Book of God's Revelation, instructing us in God's ways. I found it in The Temple!" (2 Kings 22:8 MSG). When the book is read before the king, the words distress him so much that he rips apart his robes. He sends out five messengers to locate one woman, the prophetess Huldah, who might remember what these things mean. Like Galadriel remembering the story for the fading world of Middle-earth, Huldah presages the fate the kingdom of Judah will suffer for having forgotten God's Word.

In the original book version of *The Lord of the Rings*, the wizard Gandalf identifies the ring only after researching its history in Isildur's scroll. There is an admonition not to forget our history, for such amnesia increases the spread of darkness in the world. Yet in both stories—and many more like them—hope smolders in the books of the culture, waiting to ignite the remnant against those forces that threaten to blot it out entirely. Why is memory so necessary for the flourishing of a culture, for people in general? How can remembering be more than an act of nostalgia? How can it be a virtuous endeavor against destructive powers? While the assumption in these tales is that people are supposed to retain these stories living in their memory, it is also books that restore memory to the people.

Memory as a Moral Responsibility

Throughout the Old Testament, God repeatedly commands his people to remember. If you read the Torah, you will feel like Numbers, Leviticus, and Deuteronomy repeat one another, for the repetition was needed to ensure the people did not forget the law. The Lord wants his people to pass the law down to their children, and their children's children. After relaying the Ten Commandments to the Israelites, Moses stresses the need to memorize these things:

> These commandments that I give you today are to be on your hearts. Impress them on your children. Talk about them when you sit at home and when you walk along the road, when you lie down and when you get up. Tie them as symbols on your hands and bind them on your foreheads. Write them on the doorframes of your houses and on your gates. (Deut. 6:6–9)

In our hearts, to our children, at our dinner tables, before we sleep, before we rise, all over our homes, the words of God are to be everywhere so that we remember them. To remember the words of God, we must fill the spaces of our lives with them. Only then will they be written in our hearts.

In C. S. Lewis's novel *The Silver Chair*, Aslan impresses upon a newcomer to Narnia the necessity of memory. To the young girl named Jill, Aslan gives a series of signs that will aid her in her quest: "Remember, remember, remember the Signs. Say them to yourself when you wake in the morning and when you lay down at night and when you wake in the middle of the night."[2] Of course, this line recalls Deuteronomy 6:6–9. Three times Aslan repeats the imperative, "Remember." Then he insists on remembering by the hours of the day, like the liturgy a monk would follow, repeating the Scriptures all day long. The words of God should be like the song that you cannot get out of your head, the one that you find yourself humming without meaning to, the song that you thoughtlessly tap your feet to, and that echoes from your heart and through your whole body.

When Aslan speaks to Jill, he adds a second warning about remembering these signs. On the mountaintop, the signs come directly from Aslan's mouth; they are clear and understandable. Like God speaking face-to-face with Moses on Sinai, Aslan communicates here with Jill. But when she descends, the air will thicken and confuse her so that the signs will not look the same when she encounters them on earth. "That is why it is so important to know them by heart," Aslan reminds Jill.[3] It is not enough to know the signs in her mind, they must be written on her heart. She must know them with her emotions, in her habits, and they must be practiced in how she lives—that is what it means to know them in one's heart.

In our culture, where all of history is the click of a button away, how is it that we have no space in our lives for the vocation of memory? I probably just answered my own question. We think we do not need to remember because our phones are portals to all facts and semblances of knowledge. However, for the Judaic people and the early Christian church, memory was a moral responsibility. Ivan Illich writes, "The art of memory is closely intertwined with the art of reading; one cannot be understood without the other."[4] To remember is to embody what you know, the experiences you have lived both biographically and vicariously through what you have read.

It's a proverbial truth that "you are what you eat," meaning that you will only be as healthy as the food you put into your body. But Jesus countered this assumption by saying, "It's not what goes into your mouth that defiles you; you are defiled by the words that come out of your mouth" (Matt. 15:11 NLT). In other words, what a person says or does reveals what has been digested within her and formed her. When Psyche, a character in Lewis's novel *Till We Have Faces*, approaches her execution, she mimics her teacher the Fox by recalling his catechism to her sister Orual: "You make me think I have learned the Fox's lessons better than you. Have you forgotten what we are to say to ourselves every morning?"[5] She does not fear death because she has learned her catechism by heart. Unlike Orual, who merely said the words, Psyche remembers them; they emerge from her as wisdom.

Scholars over the past few years have highlighted how Lewis was formed by the medieval literature he regularly read and taught.[6] While Protestants deem Lewis their patron saint, they have not often regarded him as a *ressourcement* writer who reintroduces modern readers to the pre-Reformation church. In *The Medieval Mind of C. S. Lewis*, Jason Baxter underscores how Lewis's knowledge of classical and medieval books could not be stopped from being embodied in his work: Lewis could not "formulate an argument, write a letter, offer a word of consolation, or weave a fictional story of his own without opening up the dam and letting all the old ideas and emotions, stored up in his memory by long reading, break forth."[7] Lewis created from what he remembered.

Memory as a Spiritual Practice

In her book *The Craft of Thought*, medievalist Mary Carruthers corrects the modern misordering of the five canons of rhetoric and points out specifically how our misconception of the relationship between invention and memory has distracted us from the real priority. In school, I learned the canons in this order: invention, organization, style, memory, delivery. In other words, you invent words on a page, arrange them, craft them to sound pretty, memorize the product, and recite it. But Carruthers points out that memory precedes invention. She writes, "The arts of memory are among the arts of thinking . . . [what] we now revere as 'imagination' and 'creativity.'"[8] The word "invention" has its root in "inventory." Carruthers returns memory to its proper position—first—among our ways of thinking, for we must remember in order to invent.[9]

Even interpretation was considered an act of invention. For the medieval thinker, one needed to focus on what she remembered to construct thoughts, to invent dialogue, to create interpretation in art or prose. "The purpose of such memorial summary is to make new compositions of gloss and interpretation," Carruthers writes. "Thus, *memoria rerum* [memory for things] is essential for literary invention; its purpose is to compose new discourse."[10] The hurdle of originality was nonexistent to the medieval mind. How could you ever invent without that which came before in your inventory? The medieval thinkers emphasized remembering as a practice essential to reading. Education for them was intended "not to become a 'living book' (by rote reiteration, the power of an idiot)," Carruthers writes, "but to become a 'living concordance,' the power of prudence and wisdom."[11] From reading, meditating, memorizing, and then interpreting the books within oneself, one could live wisely in the world.

Remembering What You Have Read

Medieval readers went about memorizing in several ways: liturgy, copying, reciting, illustrating, and mapping. Within the monastery, monks heard the Scriptures at regular hours throughout the day. In the course of a week, a monk would repeat all 150 psalms aloud. They memorized the Bible because they repeated it in their mouths, heard the words sung from their brothers' and sisters' voices, and saw the verses spread out on the page. In addition to Scripture, they would memorize the heroic tales of Alexander, the surreal metamorphoses of Ovid, or the philosophy of Aristotle by copying the texts and illuminating them. Their illustrations were not mere ornaments but served as mnemonic devices.[12] Images on the pages helped readers locate themselves within the work and chart their way like a pilgrim on a route. Similarly, we now scribble our own annotations into margins or employ underlining to aid our digestion of a book. We can find our thoughts in conversation with the book and continue moving through it with this kind of place marking.

Finally, medieval readers would build memory palaces to store what was worth remembering, constructing imaginary structures to locate various texts in places within their minds. Carruthers discusses this mnemonic, indicating how memory was a construction in the mind of the medieval: "All knowledge depends on memory, and so it is all retained in images, fictions gathered into several places and reground into new 'places' as the thinking mind draws them together."[13] Monks could imagine the monastery or chapel as a place attached to specific lines or verses, and they could outline a book onto the structure of the space. During the Stations of the Cross, for instance, faithful penitents walk a symbolic path to Calvary, tracing Jesus's steps, with verses connected to each place in the chapel. And, each week, priests would walk the sanctuary, preparing their homilies, locating sections of their sermons in specific spots within the room. When they delivered the homily from the pulpit, they would imaginatively walk that journey again in their minds, moving through their exposition. Hugh of St. Victor accomplishes a memory palace in the shape of Noah's ark and guides the reader through the structure as a way of remembering his points.

We also practice memory by rereading books over and over again. If you ask my mentor Ralph Wood whether he has read a book, he responds, "Read it? I haven't even taught it yet." Wood means that he could only say he had read a book after he had taught it, for then he would truly know it. The best books are those that demand rereading; we call these classics. Yet, as another of my teachers, Louise Cowan, has noted, "It is not enough for them to be known *about*; they need to be truly *known* in the fullness of their intimacy."[14] Cowan shares her list of those books she rereads annually: *Iliad, Oedipus Rex, Hamlet, The Divine Comedy*. These remembered works then constitute her vision. What is remembered is what is read. We should take care to remember what we have loved from a book while taking heart that even what is forgotten has formed us.

Exercises in memory are being incorporated more into education as people are realizing the necessity of this storehouse of wisdom that medieval readers took for granted. In classical education, kindergartners through seniors in high school memorize large chunks of text, multiplication tables, or the periodic table of elements, for instance, to construct their storehouse. They fill their reservoir with poems by Phillis Wheatley, Robert Frost, Petrarch, or Anna Akhmatova. They recite them at regular intervals throughout the year. When I taught fourth grade, each student memorized a section from a Shakespearean play. I listened to the students practice these recitations each day, and by the end of the term, I knew Portia's speech, parts of the St. Crispin's Day speech, and Hamlet's monologue. It is not enough to memorize a weekly Bible verse; we need to practice memorizing speeches and poems and texts that we never want to be lost.

In the fourteenth century, Marie de France composed little poetic stories to recite at the court of the king and queen of England in order that good things may not be forgotten. She defends the act of storytelling at the conclusion of her recitation: "The ancient courtly Bretons composed a lay to be remembered, so that it should not be forgotten."[15] While that sentence may sound redundant, Marie is emphasizing that the truth of the story is best remembered not as a concise message but in the form of the story itself. We remember the message best through the narrative. She argues that these stories will help others "avoid future mistakes," "guard against vice," and "rid [themselves] of great suffering."[16] In this case, by composing a brief romance in poetic form, Marie shares with her audience the moral truths that ought not to be lost.

Cultural Memory

At the conclusion of Ray Bradbury's popular novel *Fahrenheit 451*, some of the firemen revolt, memorizing the books before they burn them. They identify themselves by the books composed within their memory: "We are all bits and pieces of history and literature and international law, Byron, Tom Paine, Machiavelli or Christ, it's here. And the hour's late. And the war's begun. And we are out here. . . . We are model citizens, in our own way; we walk the old tracks."[17] As the firemen walk out into the world and away from the burning city behind them, they determine to do one important thing: "We're remembering. That's where we'll win out in the long run."[18] To re-member is to put the body back together again; remembering is an embodied practice, as Bradbury illustrates in this novel. These embodied memory keepers are determined to "pass the books [that they have memorized] on to [their] children by word of mouth and let [their] children wait."[19] For the fire not to destroy civilization, these firemen have realized that they must imagine it as a cleansing fire, one that opens up the opportunity to start again.[20]

Without a shared cultural memory, we are divided and fractured from one another. We talk past one another instead of converse with one another. "When you can assume that your audience holds the same beliefs you do, you can relax a little and use more normal means of talking to it; when you have to assume that it does not, then you have to make your vision apparent by shock," Flannery O'Connor writes.[21] If we begin with a shared cultural memory, we can go deeper. Without such common beliefs, we have to push our audience to even reach square one in our discussion. Although we cannot consider the tradition as a confined product to be passed on to the next generation, we need to cherish the tradition by keeping "the best that has been thought and said," in Matthew Arnold's phrase, alive within us by repeated reading and engagement.

BOOKMARK 4

◆———◆

Reading like Dorothy L. Sayers

The BBC aired Dorothy L. Sayers's drama about the life of Jesus Christ, *The Man Born to Be King*, beginning on December 21, 1941. On that same day, three submarines—British, Dutch, and German—were torpedoed and sunk, the Japanese invaded the Philippines, and the Germans began murdering inmates at Bogdanovka concentration camp in Ukraine. In the midst of the tragedies of World War II, mere weeks after the Americans suffered the attack on Pearl Harbor, British citizens were listening to the Gospels being spoken in contemporary language through their radios and into their homes. Imagine the immense balm to the souls of the fearful Londoners, with the assuring words drawn from the Gospels drowning out the sirens and German planes above them. One of the wise men says to Mary, who has recently given birth to Jesus, "Fear is our daily companion. . . . But all this we could bear if we knew that we did not suffer in vain; that God was beside us in the struggle, sharing in the miseries of His own world."[1] Through her life and work, Sayers shows us how to be the best kind of reader, and she brings what she reads to bear on her current world. She herself loved books, the Bible first of all, but also Dante and *The Song of Roland* and Agatha Christie novels. For Sayers, created works were evidence of a living God, a Creator still at work in his creation.

Knowing and Sharing the Gospels through Literature

Sayers's radio plays were aired nearly a century before *The Passion of the Christ* film or *The Chosen* series, so twenty-first-century readers may not realize the extreme act of subversion on Sayers's part to reimagine the life of Jesus Christ for a contemporary audience. Portraying the Trinity on stage was illegal in Britain, but performing the Gospels in radio form provided a loophole. In the introduction to the published version of the plays, Sayers explains that writing the drama was "a quite new experiment, undertaken in the face of a good deal of prejudice, and in the absence of any adequate standards of comparison."[2] When Sayers read publicly from her forthcoming play cycle, magazines lit up with headlines: "BBC Life of Christ Play in U.S. Slang" and "Gangterisms in Bible Play."[3] Religious organizations attacked her for blaspheming the Gospels. As the director-general of the BBC put it, "Two shocks broke on us this past week: Pearl Harbor and *The Man Born to Be King*."[4] Few conceived that Sayers may have been employing literature as a medium of evangelism. While she would have distanced herself from that way of labeling her work, Sayers was sharing the good news of God through a literary form.

For Sayers—as for many twentieth-century converts to Christianity—literature turned her to the church. Although Sayers was raised in a Christian family, she compartmentalized the role of faith in her life. Not until she read G. K. Chesterton's novel *The Napoleon of Notting Hill* did Sayers discover a love for the church in which her parents had raised her. In the preface to Chesterton's play *The Surprise*, Sayers writes of the great writer, "To the young people of my generation, G. K. C. [Chesterton] was a kind of Christian liberator. Like a beneficent bomb, he blew out of the Church a quantity of stained glass of a very poor period, and let in gusts of fresh air."[5]

In a similar way to how Chesterton revived Sayers's dry faith, George MacDonald's novels moved the young atheist C. S. Lewis to become a Christian. Likewise, the novelist Fyodor Dostoevsky compelled Walker Percy to convert to Catholicism, and his novels returned the former Communist Aleksandr Solzhenitsyn to the Russian Orthodox Church. The Nobel Prize–winning novelist Sigrid Undset was converted not only by Chesterton but also by the novelist Robert Hugh Benson. The philosopher and nun Edith Stein used to give Undset's novels to new novices in her Carmelite order to increase their desire for holiness. For innumerable souls, fiction has proved to be a powerful vehicle for Christian conversion.

However, Sayers never would have written what we now label "Christian fiction," because she insisted on an inextricable relationship between dogma and drama. Much of what is branded as Christian fiction shows little care for or dedication to aesthetics. Form has been severed from content, with the emphasis falling on the latter. Such a dichotomy denies the reality of our theology. If we are embodied souls, if the Word has become flesh, if the letter is bound with the spirit, then we cannot create convincing messages with faulty forms. Sayers extends this claim further: "For a work of art that is not good and true *in art* is not good or true in any other respect, and it is useless for any purpose whatsoever—even for edification—because it is a lie."[6] Without the requisite drama, the dogma becomes less than impotent; it becomes mendacious.

In her introduction to the play, Sayers denounces artists who excuse their lack of craft while espousing high devotion to their religion. "A loose and sentimental theology begets loose and sentimental art-forms," Sayers writes. She knew that the Scriptures could withstand the test of being adapted into drama. "Nothing so glaringly exposes inconsistencies in a character, a story, or a philosophy as to put it upon the stage and allow it to speak for itself," Sayers insists.[7] Her dramatization of the Gospels proves the strength of the truthfulness of their story. Rather than being accused of blasphemy, Sayers should be exalted as performing apologetics through art. She exhibits for readers how to read the Gospels with a literary eye and how that lens illuminates the authenticity of the story.

Defamiliarization

What scandalized Sayers's listeners after they initially heard *The Man Born to Be King* was the contemporary and common language used by the biblical characters. The King James Version had been so familiar to British churchgoers that Sayers's rendering verses into plain style sounded irreverent. Sayers calls out this obsessive dedication to the King James translation for what it is—idolatry. Readers were holding the words sacrosanct, but not the words of the Greek original, not the authentic documents, "but to every syllable of a translation made three hundred years ago (and that not always with perfect accuracy) in an idiom so old-fashioned that, even as English, it is often obscure to us or positively misleading."[8] Sayers points out how we become more attached to what is familiar than devoted to what is true.

When I was first dating my husband, he told me that the King James was the most accurate version of the Bible. "According to whom?" I inquired. Although he had no answer to give, he felt certain of it. His emotional ties to that translation were strong, and his church community had insisted the KJV was the authentic and most authoritative version. Similar protests met Eugene Peterson when he translated *The Message* into common English, a seemingly heretical act; some have protested even calling it a Bible. Yet Peterson defends his choices as aligned with the original Koine Greek, and in keeping with the early translators such as Jerome, Tyndale, and Luther.[9] They were all trying to capture the common speech of the Bible, for it was written in accessible and widely used, idiomatic forms of Greek. It was never meant to be petrified into one particular translation.

By translating from the common language of the original Greek Scriptures, Sayers hoped that her artistic adaptation of the Gospels would shock listeners into recognizing the truth of the story. "God was executed by people painfully like us," Sayers laments. "If you show people that, they are shocked. So they should be."[10] To that end, Sayers tore off the costume of the sixteenth-century idioms and brought us face-to-face with ourselves in the story. "*We* played the parts in that tragedy, nineteen and a half centuries since, and perhaps are playing them today, in the same good faith and in the same ironic ignorance," Sayers writes.[11] Through her artistic engagement with the Scriptures, Sayers defamiliarizes the narrative and its verses, which may have become so well-known as to no longer be heard.

We have been conditioned by our churches and culture to read Scripture in certain ways, some of those ways lovely and accurate, but others that cloud our knowledge of the Scriptures from their real meaning and significance. "Let us, in heaven's name, drag out the divine drama from under the dreadful accumulation of slipshod thinking and trashy sentiment," Sayers contends.[12] She believed in the necessity of defamiliarization to weed out the heresy from the fruitful truth. Literature—poetry, narratives, drama—acts as a defamiliarizing agent for Scripture. Granted, other art can also play this role, but for the sake of this discussion, how does literature accomplish this defamiliarization well? Great literature recasts the known into a different setting or form or language so that we may see and hear the truth as it is.

British poet and reverend Malcolm Guite invested years writing sonnets every time he preached a sermon. Responding to the church calendar's designated Scriptures, Guite submitted himself to crafting sonnets from those verses given. If on one

Sunday, for instance, Ezekiel 12:1–2 and Matthew 13:9–17 were read, then Guite recited his verse: "How hard to hear the things I think I know, / To peel aside the thin familiar film."[13] His sonnet addresses the hardness that occurs to our hearts when we assume we already know what is being said. He describes defamiliarization as peeling aside the familiar. This disclosure becomes, in the remainder of the sonnet, reimagined as another raising of Lazarus from the dead. For every one of us to whom the Scriptures sound like empty words falling on our deaf ears, Guite echoes Jesus's call, "Lazarus, come forth!" His sonnet both clarifies the necessity of defamiliarization as a biblical practice and acts as a resource to defamiliarize us with those verses and that story.

Great authors have often drawn on biblical tropes or language as a way of defamiliarizing readers with the truth of Scripture. Despite the fact that many first-time readers of Flannery O'Connor cannot process what she is up to, her short stories produce similar defamiliarization. Many scholars have contended that her narratives act as a "kind of *rewriting* of Scripture, intended not to replace the sacred text but to restate its ancient truths in her own time and her own way for her own, largely unbelieving audience."[14] She assumed her readers would share her familiarity with the Bible, so reading her stories would remind them of the reality and power in what the Scriptures said. Yet, a story or poem need not retell the Scriptures to defamiliarize us with the spiritual realities revealed to us in the Word.

What's in a Word?

Sayers herself enjoyed the luxury of knowing the original languages of the Bible, so she could read the source fresh. As a translator, she could renew people's appreciation of works besides Scripture that may have sounded dated or may have lost their real presence for readers. "The passion for verse-translation is a kind of congenital disease," Sayers confessed in a talk on the subject. "I have suffered from it all my life."[15] Fluent in French at an early age, Sayers received a scholarship to Somerville College at Oxford, where she earned a first in modern languages and medieval literature (though degrees were not officially granted to women until almost a decade later). When Sayers determined to translate Dante's *The Divine Comedy*, her audience recoiled at the idea that their favorite, bestselling mystery novelist could translate medieval Italian. In parallel, perhaps it would be like twenty-first-century readers hearing that John Grisham was producing a verse translation of Chaucer's *Canterbury Tales*. In spite of the protests, Sayers defended her translation as yet another opportunity to bring literature to life for readers.

In 1944, as British civilians hid regularly in air-raid shelters, Sayers grabbed a book to pass the time. She picked up *The Divine Comedy*. Her friend Charles Williams had raved about the poem, but she herself had never read it. She writes to Williams, "I was prepared to find him a GREAT POET and, of course, a GREAT RELIGIOUS POET, all in solemn capital letters; but I was not prepared to find him good company, and I was certainly not prepared to find myself continually saying with a chuckle, 'Dear, funny Dante!'"[16] In Dante, Sayers had found a friend. That night in the air-raid shelter, she enjoyed his company. As much as she learned from him—as we all do from good friends—Sayers saw in Dante someone much like herself.

Sayers had reinvigorated the Scriptures for listeners in the early 1940s with her radio plays, and now she was to reintroduce readers to a fourteenth-century Italian epic. As a translator, Sayers models for us how to read closely and well, how to put stories and verse into our own words, and how to love the text before us. A translator does not merely read about a book, check out the SparkNotes, or flip through the pages once and set it down. Rather, a translator must fulfill what Cowan says of all readers in regard to great texts: know the book intimately; take it in and savor it.

On the effort of translating, Sayers reminds poets to seek only those authors with whom they identify. She writes, "Between poet and translator there needs to be that kind of relation that exists between a tiger and a cat. The cat is very much smaller than the tiger, but there are things she instinctively knows about tigers which the elephant cannot know."[17] In other words, the translator must read not only the words on the page but also as though she is the author and the reader: like a playwright who must perform the roles of the actors while imagining the effects on the audience. From her experience with the stage, Sayers knew how to translate well. In order for Sayers to translate another's poem, she needed to enter the mind of the author and share the author's way of reading and translating reality.

By translating, Sayers could bring an old work to life for contemporary and future readers. "All great works should be retranslated from time to time," Sayers suggests, else we must "wrestle with two strange frames of discourse instead of one."[18] How many students have failed to enjoy *The Divine Comedy* because they read Henry Wadsworth Longfellow's Victorian translation? If we do not retranslate works from the past, we face the additional obstacle, for example, of a nineteenth-century translation as well as the hurdle of a fourteenth-century Italian epic. Although Sayers left *Paradiso* uncompleted at her death, her translation of *The Divine Comedy* is considered by some to be her most monumental achievement.

Read as Sayers Translates

For those of us who are not destined to be translators, what can we learn about how to read from this Christian scholar and her practice of translation? In Sayers the translator, we see a woman participating in redemptive, kingdom work. What was undone at the tower of Babel by human pride is redeemed by Pentecost: human beings divided by many different languages were enabled by the Holy Spirit to understand one another's speech. Every time we attend to languages other than our first language, we are participating in redemptive work. There is always time to listen to other languages and consider them, even if you consider yourself too old to become fluent in a new language. When we hear the words of another language, our minds are opened to a way of imagining what the words signify that is different from what our limited vocabulary can encompass.

Consider Julia Alvarez's "Bilingual Sestina," in which she highlights the beauty and frustrations of two tongues, of knowing the world through two languages. She opens her poem, "Some things I have to say aren't getting said / in this snowy, blonde, blue-eyed, gum chewing English."[19] Alvarez reveals the intimate connection between words and the way we think, see, and know our world. Without the aid of her first language, Spanish, she cannot say what she means. Some ideas are simply untranslatable, pointing to the incomprehensibility of this world given to us by God and the ineffability of God himself. When we hear translators explain the challenges of moving from Italian to English or English to Spanish, we receive a glimmer of the truth that the world cannot be known only by ourselves. We once again remember that we need other voices and other eyes to know what we are missing.

In his exploration of the evolution of human language, Owen Barfield indicates how radically different human beings have conceived of words across time and place. In ancient Greek culture, for instance, one could not "grow a beard." The word used would be "foamed." Poetic metaphors were "a bedrock element in the Greek language," so much so that the Greeks did not consider words as referential but existential.[20] Words not only show how a culture thinks, but they reveal the lens through which a culture is created. This is why J. R. R. Tolkien established the languages of the people of Middle-earth before he wrote *The Lord of the Rings*. The languages produced the tale. How much are we missing about the meaning of a story if we do not seek to know at least the key words within the original language of a text? If it was recommended by the early church writers for Christians to possess some smattering of Greek and Hebrew to understand Scripture, it should behoove us, as it did Sayers, to learn some Italian to understand Dante. Or to grasp a bit of Russian to read Dostoevsky, Bulgakov, Solzhenitsyn. To learn at least some Spanish, French, Norwegian, Chinese to be able to unravel those texts in their original languages.

By seeing translators at work, we realize that reading must begin in loving the words and is only fulfilled when we share what we love. Google Translate cannot accomplish that love for the words. Discussing Sarah Ruden's translation of the Gospels, Scot McKnight writes, "If translators are priests, then some mediate the text, the author, and that world better than others. . . . A translator collaborates with the text and her readers."[21] A translation recognizes the communal nature of reading, the relationship between text, author, and reader. Translations encourage conversation, connection, and unity across the gap of differing tongues, and translators perform a service to others, for they themselves are not required to share what they have read. Rather, translators attempt a new rendering of the work flowing from their joy and love for the text.

Moreover, translators must find themselves at home in another's text rather than a mere stranger trespassing through another's territory. Translators become good models for how to identify with and empathize with authors rather than set oneself against them with either skepticism at best or antagonism at worst. In his book *A Preface to Paradise Lost*, C. S. Lewis advises readers, "Instead of stripping the knight of his armor you can try to put his armor on yourself." Rather than try to force ancient Greek writings to meet our standards, we should try to imagine ourselves in that world. Lewis explains, "To enjoy our full humanity, we ought, so far as possible, to contain within us potentially at all times, and on occasion to actualize, all the modes of feeling and thinking through which [the human] has passed."[22] Like the Holy Spirit at Pentecost, who brought people together not by synthesizing all languages into one language or erasing all differences but by uniting us in our differences, so too these books, written in separate tongues across various times and cultures, reveal to us our full, shared humanity.

In Defense of Fiction

Sayers wrote a poem titled "The Maker" about the necessity of freedom for the artist, for the creation, and for the reader. For Sayers, the Trinity participated in the creation of art as much as in its reception. In her poem, she plays out a dialogue between the Architect, the Craftsman, and the Stone. Each knows its role and its part, designated by its nature. Then the poem turns: "The work no master may subject / Save He to whom the whole is known / Being Himself the Architect, the Craftsman and the Corner-stone."[23] Sayers shows in this poem how the Lord is at work in all our work, whether adapting Bible stories to dramas, translating epic poems, or writing detective novels. The artist is required to subject the work to God, and the reader is entrusted with reading that work well.

Most readers do not appreciate how good detective fiction is often theology in narrative. In a good detective story, the artist must acknowledge the fallenness of the world—often manifest in human beings' proclivity toward violence and death, symptomatic of our sinfulness. As G. K. Chesterton showed in his Father Brown series, mystery stories reveal the potential for murder in every human heart. But then justice steps in. The riddle is solved, and the detective delivers justice. The reader experiences catharsis: all shall be well. In writing these "framed lies,"[24] Sayers told stories in which characters exhibited liberty, stories that paradoxically told the truth about the world. For those who decry fiction as nothing but illusion, detective stories test our deceitful hearts to seek out the truth. Sayers writes, "Any fool can tell a lie, and any fool can believe it; but the right method is to tell the *truth* in such a way that the intelligent reader is seduced into telling the lie for himself."[25] Our mendacious nature is held up before our eyes, and we are guilty of deceiving ourselves in the reading. Through their fictional guise, detective stories not only show us our evil hearts, they inculcate in readers a desire for truth.

Christians have been suspicious of fiction for a long time. Is it not just lies dressed up for our amusement that tempt us away from the serious business of morals and doing good in the world? My students are eager to go and change the world, so they initially begrudge the time required in my class to sit and chatter about novels—until we read them together. Give me ten minutes with the most hesitant of Christian readers, and I will invite them to fall in love with God through fiction.

Even a century ago, Sayers faced this antagonism toward her call to write detective stories. Considered either a lovely pastime or a wayward hobby, reading detective fiction did not attract a line of pastors to her door for her theological wisdom. Nor did Sayers herself begin writing detective novels with any explicitly righteous motivation. She merely needed to make money, and she enjoyed the stories. Sayers was so successful as a detective novelist that she eventually became president of the Detection Club in London, founded by Chesterton and led later by Agatha Christie. C. S. Lewis said Sayers was the first famous person to ever write him. For many in the early twentieth-century English-speaking world, Sayers's detective Lord Peter Wimsey was a household name. They awaited the next Wimsey novel the way nineteenth-century readers looked for the next Sherlock Holmes. Despite her deep Christian beliefs, Sayers protected the agnosticism of her protagonist. When readers tried to convince her to convert Wimsey, she upheld his free will: "You shall not impose either your will or mine upon my creature. He is what he is, I will work no irrelevant miracles upon him, either for propaganda, or to curry favour, or to establish the consistency of my own principles. He exists in his own right and not to please you. Hands off."[26] We hear the artist in imitation of her Creator, uplifting the freedom of his creatures to love and choose him, or not. Sayers was not the kind of detective novelist who forced her characters, her readers, or the literary game to suit others.

The question about detective fiction must be posed of all fiction: How much does the story tell the truth about the world? Does it highlight the patterns of reality, thread the themes together in such a way that we would not have seen it before? I do not need all art to be high art, but I do want all art to strive to be art.[27] If fiction is art, whether those stories be detective bestsellers or epics or romances, they should tell the truth about the world. Maybe not plainly—hence Sayers's proclivity for framing lies. Maybe in fiction the truth is slant. But good fiction does tell the truth, the highest truth.

Conclusion

I n the midst of chaos and noise, the call to read may sound silly. Don't we need to be improving the world? Fighting injustice? Stopping wars, curing illness, feeding the poor? Yes, of course. I believe in the need for beautification, revolution, and acts of mercy. However, we must imagine the ends that we are fighting for. Reading well encourages us to join these impermanent battles, to see the good causes from the evil machinations, and to know truth from falsehood. A pious person who spends time reading great books well has more resources needed to act wisely in an impious age. Opening a book should not be the final goal but the invitation to a broader vision.

In a world that tries to convince us that we are computers or animals, that treats us like automatons or worker bees, what better protest than the reading life? If we are to be fully human, we must practice human acts—civility, creativity, contemplation, charity. Such practice may be gained from listening to a dissenting opinion in a book. For example, in March 2022, I read a biography of Vladimir Putin to try to make sense of what was happening in Ukraine.[1] Or, when comforting a mother who had recently miscarried, I read Dana Gioia's poem "Planting a Sequoia" and recalled the burial of my unborn son beneath our backyard trees.[2] We read for knowledge, for comfort, for joy. Our family has listened to Charles Dickens performed by the BBC on Audible so many times that our children perform their own version in costumes in the living room.

Since the early church, Christians have prized words. We should continue to be those weirdos who spend less time in the virtual ether and more time in stories, poetry, and drama. The reading life is not isolated or hermetic. Those who have experienced memorable literature classes or book clubs or family read-aloud time recognize the joy of reading in community; it bonds family and friends and neighbors in unquantifiable ways. By reading in concert, we hand on cultural memory, we draw people into shared experiences, and we unify diverse voices in a beautiful harmony. The reading life is a life that loves the Word. A reader refuses to be absorbed by the world yet is still in the world. Christians are called to be the most human among us— readers—those who have not forgotten what it means to be a bookish people, for in the beginning was the Word, and in the end is the book of life.

Acknowledgments

First and foremost, I need to acknowledge those who taught me how to read well: Michael Gose, David Lyle Jeffrey, Ralph C. Wood, Dana Gioia, Sarah Jane Murray, and many others. Without their friendship and guidance, I would not have been able to write this book. Also thank you to those who taught me through their books, especially Alan Jacobs, from whom I learn every time I read his work.

Thank you to the University of Dallas, which hosted my scholarship and writing from 2020 to 2022 and which provided me the chance to lead a graduate seminar "The Art of Reading" in 2021. I am especially grateful to Matt Post for the ingenuity of creating the position at the university, to President Jonathan J. Sanford for supporting it, and to Bainard Cowan, who brought me to the Cowan Archives, granted me the use of his mother's name as the title of my position, and is a saint in process whom I'm blessed to call friend.

As the ideas were germinating, I was able to share them in my classroom at John Brown University and later at the Well-Read Mom's Tenth Anniversary event at Circe National Conference, as well as at other universities and classical schools where friends, parents, and teachers asked great questions and led me to seek better answers.

To those who brought the book to Brazos Press—my agent Keely Boeving and my editor Bob Hosack—thank you so much for seeing the worth of this book before it came to be. My thanks to Jeff Reimer and Eric Salo for their meticulous editing: thank you for not letting me say anything stupid or unclear.

To the friends who read the drafts before the book was published—thank you for taking the time. Also, thank you to my friends who have gathered for book club; it has been such a gift to me to spend our time sharing and talking about what we love to read.

Finally, my husband gave me the time to write on weekends and in the evenings after our kids were asleep—thank you for supporting my vocation. I hope books like this one compel the next generation, including our children, to be people of the book.

Appendix A

Twofold Reading of Flannery O'Connor's "The River"

To practice how to read literature literally and spiritually, let's walk through Flannery O'Connor's short story "The River." If you have not yet read it, I encourage you, as my teacher Ralph Wood says, "Get thee to the bookstore!" Pick up a copy of O'Connor's *Complete Stories* and read the story all the way through. "The River" begins with a small boy of indeterminate age—four or five—being shoved into a plaid coat by his father. On the literal level, this boy is being pushed around by his parents; they objectify him and treat him thoughtlessly. By not buttoning the coat correctly, the father has made it difficult for the boy, who we soon learn is called Harry Ashfield, to function. Drawing from our physical senses, we notice the Ashfields' living room is dark, the father is in his bathrobe, there is the smell of dead cigarette butts and the sound of change for the bus dropping from one hand to another. Our introduction to the literal story places us in a concrete world that we can imagine fully; it is real: we can see, smell, and hear that reality.

The plot of the story is fairly simple, and, like many of O'Connor's stories, the plot alone would not necessarily entice someone to read it. Mrs. Connin cares for Harry Ashfield over the course of one day because his parents are hungover from the night before. Harry introduces himself to his sitter as "Bevel" after Mrs. Connin refers to an evangelist preacher by that name. He hears the story of Jesus for the first time in a Golden Book he finds at Mrs. Connin's home. Then he is baptized in a river by the real Bevel Summers, who tells him to choose between "Jesus and the devil." An injured heckler named Mr. Paradise sits on the roof of his car watching the baptisms and mocking the parade of penitents. Mrs. Connin returns Bevel/Harry to his home. She is so mortified by the careless parenting of the Ashfields that she refuses to accept money for caring for the boy. He goes to sleep feeling as though he now matters and wakes up determined to return to that place where he "counted." When he travels to the river, no one is there except Mr. Paradise, who lurks behind him with candy in his pocket. Harry walks into the river, eager to be taken to that other kingdom of which the preacher spoke. Mr. Paradise attempts unsuccessfully to retrieve him from the river, and Harry's prayers are answered, as he drowns.

After reading the story, we may be profoundly discontented by its literal sense: a neglected child drowns himself. The story demands a spiritual reality for the reader to make sense of what she just experienced, and therein lies its power. As a Catholic writer familiar with her tradition, O'Connor knew the four senses of Scripture, and she wanted to translate them into fiction. She wanted her readers to practice moving through the literal sense toward spiritual import. To accomplish this goal for her very literal, primarily Protestant audience, O'Connor wrote stories that, when read *only literally*, confounded her readers.

In an explanation of "A Good Man Is Hard to Find," O'Connor clarifies the literal and spiritual way of reading her work that may be applied to all of her stories. She says,

A good story is literal in the same sense that a child's drawing is literal. When a child draws, he doesn't intend to distort but to set down exactly what he sees, and as his gaze is direct, he sees the lines that create motion. Now the lines of motion that interest the writer are usually invisible. They are lines of spiritual motion. And in this story you should be on the lookout for such things as the action of grace.[1]

Although readers mistakenly describe O'Connor's work as grotesque, she does not consider her work as participating in this aesthetic, one that distorts for the sake of illustrating the strangeness of life. What appears to be grotesque in her stories is a literal rendering of reality, but the literal world always carries a second sense, whether or not we acknowledge it. All of matter possesses spirit; reality itself is twofold, as Augustine indicates. Therefore, we must seek the action of grace in O'Connor's stories to illuminate the mystery that has caused the literal to appear scandalous before our eyes. We must learn to read spiritually.

We know that O'Connor, like Dorothy L. Sayers and other mid-twentieth-century Christian writers, read Dante and studied early Christian ways of reading Scripture. Many scholars have labeled O'Connor's aesthetic "incarnational" or "sacramental" because of the spiritual meaning latent in all her stories. When we read "The River" as one example, we should begin with the title. How can we meditate on the meaning of a river? There are several dozen biblical passages that refer to rivers, starting with those that flow out of Eden to water the garden (Gen. 2:10), to the river of life in Revelation 22:1. When Moses curses Pharaoh to prove God's strength, he turns the Nile River into blood (Exod. 7:20). After Moses's passing, Joshua takes command of the Israelites, and God proves his presence by parting the Jordan River.[2] As Elijah passes his mantle to Elisha, he too parts the Jordan River before he is taken up into heaven (2 Sam. 17:15–22). In this same river, hundreds of years later, John will baptize his cousin Jesus of Nazareth (Matt. 3:13). For hundreds of years in the church's tradition, rivers have been interpreted as a source of life, freedom from oppression, God's presence, and his blessing on his chosen people. Only by meditating on the spiritual import of the river does Bevel's drowning make any sense.

The story ends with Harry/Bevel seeking "the Kingdom of Christ" in the river; he wants to count. As the boy drowns, O'Connor lets us experience his perspective: he "knew that he was getting somewhere, all his fury and fear left him."[3] Unlike how we saw Harry at the beginning of this story, being objectified by his family and ignored as though he did not matter, the boy experiences peace and a sense of purpose in the guidance of the river. Literally, the river is leading him to death, but this death will empty out into the river of life, where there will be no more anger or fear. In the Catholic Church, the catechumen receives a new name after baptism. This follows the biblical tradition of Abram becoming Abraham or Saul becoming Paul once chosen by God. Although the young boy merely lied about his name being Bevel, it becomes his new name from the narrator in the final paragraphs of the story. He has been baptized with a new name.

Readers of O'Connor find her horrifying, often because we are accustomed to the primacy of the physical world and empirical reality as the location of plot and progress. Yet, in O'Connor's world, the spiritual sense is brought to the surface of her stories. While we profess that spiritual reality trumps worldly reason, we live so much of our lives—and so often read—as though it is the other way around. Books like Dante's *The Divine Comedy*, C. S. Lewis's *Perelandra*, and O'Connor's *Complete Stories* challenge us to image the spiritual sense of things. In a letter, O'Connor defends the spiritual meaning of her work: "For me it is the virgin birth, the Incarnation, the resurrection which are the true laws of the flesh and the physical. Death, decay, destruction are the suspension of these laws."[4] To read "The River," for instance, as though death is the final end of the boy is to negate the resurrection.

The death of Harry/Bevel is tragic, and we cannot discount that horror. His grievous end should not be overlooked, but we must remember that the story is a story. It is a parable of sorts that tests what we believe. The reality is that children die all the time, a reality which is painful, heart-wrenching, and impossible to make sense of. O'Connor's story observes such a tragedy and asks the reader, "Do you believe that God could redeem even the worst of circumstances?" Harry/Bevel did not have to die, but he did. Can God redeem even something as horrible as the needless death of a child? This is what O'Connor's stories ask of our hearts, to attend to this question and reaffirm our belief as we stand before a page of startling horror. If we are to make sense of "The River," or any of O'Connor's stories, her way of writing demands a spiritual reading.

Appendix B

Frequently Asked Questions

1. How do you know whether a book is a good book?
Preference is not the same thing as judgment. We may like (prefer) books that are not "good" in any aesthetic, moral, or veracious sense. However, if we are wanting to judge whether a book is worth our time, we should ask three questions of the book that have to do with whether it is True, Good, or Beautiful: Does the book accord with reality (Truth)? Would living out the book result in wisdom (Good)? Do the sentences or words of the book bear scrutiny and evoke pleasure (Beauty)? If the book answers yes to any one of those questions, there is something worth reading in that book.

C. S. Lewis said to avoid the heresy of elitism when it comes to what you read. Do not assume a book is great just because all the experts say so. On the other side, experts should not assume that a book that seems unliterary must be worthless. If a person genuinely *loves* a book that an expert finds distasteful, it probably deserves a second consideration. When choosing books for your family, you should enjoy reading the book aloud together. A book that cannot be read aloud with pleasure (and read repeatedly with the same pleasure!) may not be worth reading.

2. How do you choose what to read next?

I believe that books are like people: God brings us the right friends at the right times, and so the right book will meet us at the right time. Some books sit for a long while on my shelf—some still have not been read after a decade. However, I wait for the time that I am supposed to read the book. When I was young, I would choose whatever the librarian suggested, or the bookstore staff picks, or friends' enthusiastic recommendations. Many times, we do the same: we read what is chosen for book club, what is placed on the front shelf at the brick-and-mortar store, what online algorithms push forward as suggested reading.

While there is nothing wrong with reading twaddle, it is much like eating dessert. If your whole diet is composed of such stuff, your soul might vomit at some point. Instead, choose more meats and vegetables—more books that are challenging and demanding but nourishing—over the ones that go down easy and contain little substance. C. S. Lewis recommends reading three old books for every new one. In addition, I'd recommend at least three literary books for every nonliterary choice.

There is also much to be said about reading with themes, guidelines, or certain commitments. For instance, I know a friend on social media who decided to read only books by authors of color for one year. I've considered spending a year reading only books older than myself. Many people want to read ten classics a year or five biographies a year or so on. When I teach courses or have a book idea, I read a selection of novels, history, or philosophy that all pertain to a theme. There is no right way to pursue the next book to read. Do not be afraid to not finish a book if it is not worthwhile. But be courageous enough to push on if you set your mind to completing it. Quoting John Milton, Karen Swallow Prior has reminded us, "Read promiscuously."[1]

3. How should I mark up my book to get to know it well?

Depending on your goal for a book, I recommend underlining the unforgettable lines, placing question marks in the margins of confusing or unsettling ideas, and using asterisks if a passage demands to be reread later. When I want to think deeply about a book, I ask about the author's intentions, the expected audience, and the kind of genre/text I'm reading. Your basic questions about the rhetorical situation help enlighten you to a text's purpose and meaning: How is the author presenting herself? How is she eliciting audience engagement? What sections of the text are most effective or persuasive or moving? As you attend to the content, do not overlook the form. Literature, especially poetry, blesses us with new vocabulary, a better way of naming the things we see. Circle lovely words; highlight striking phrases; imitate powerful sentences with your own content. Discover the beauty of the style and relish it.

4. What are some ways to find time to read more?

We live in the age of the tyranny of the screen, not to mention in a culture that prizes utility, relevance, and efficiency, all of which are incompatible with the reading life. First, we have to be aggressive in turning off the screens. To overcome the temptation from my smartphone, I removed social media apps, limited my Gmail app to one hour, and gave my husband control of my password. In our house, we do Friday movie nights, occasionally Saturday morning cartoons, and limit other shows or movies to road trips or special situations. Each family will have to create what works best for them for decreasing time on screens. After you remove the time wasted on technology, you may find more time available for reading. You can bring a book with you wherever you go, so you can read for a few minutes rather than dally on your device. Read on the plane or listen to an audiobook when you travel. Every morning, I aim to read the Bible, and every night, I read before I go to sleep—even if it's only one poem or one page. For accountability and to enjoy the book communally, start a monthly book club or lead a Sunday school class on a book.

5. Why do the Catholics have all the good literature?

To answer this question well would require a whole book, but here's a brief response that skims the surface of the issue. Because the twofold—or fourfold—way of reading became suspect during the Reformation, creative artists and writers distanced themselves from a sacramental aesthetic. Ideas and words became the tools of the Protestant imagination. However, the novel may also have been the genre invented by the Protestants, with its turn toward the interior self and its focus on the personal change of a singular character. When you compare Protestant to Catholic writing, you will see a greater emphasis on preaching, exposition, and natural beauty in the former; whereas the Catholic imagination prioritizes the things that signify as well as the grit and grime of the broken world in process of redemption. Thankfully, the twenty-first century has seen a renewed focus on imagination and works of the imagination in both Protestant and Catholic churches and a healthy ecumenism for sharing our great literature with one another.

Appendix C

Reading Lists of Great Books

Since many of these books are available from different publishers, I've provided that information only when a specific edition is recommended.

The Nursery (Ages 2–7)

The key for young readers is beautiful illustrations. Avoid stories written based on movies (especially those that are sequels to beloved films), which tend to be what Charlotte Mason calls "twaddle."

Aesop. *Aesop's Fables.*

Andersen, Hans Christian. *Fairy Tales.*

Arabian Nights. There are two classic translations, one expurgated for children by Andrew Lang, the other unabridged by Richard Burton.

Beaty, Andrea. The Questioneers series, illustrated by David Roberts (Abrams Books for Young Readers).

Belloc, Hilaire. *The Bad Child's Book of Beasts*; *Cautionary Tales.*

Berenstain, Stan, and Jan Berenstain. All of them.[1]

Boynton, Sandra. *Dinosaur Dance!*, and all of the others!

Brett, Jan. *Trouble with Trolls*; *The Mitten*; *Berlioz the Bear*.

Carle, Eric. *The Very Hungry Caterpillar* and all his other books.

Carroll, Lewis. *Alice's Adventures in Wonderland*; *Through the Looking-Glass*.

Child, Lauren. *The New Small Person*; *I Will Never Not Ever Eat a Tomato*, and all the rest.

Collodi, Carlo. *Pinocchio*.

Cooney, Barbara. *Miss Rumphius*; *Roxaboxen*.

Cronin, Doreen. Click Clack series; *Diary of a Worm*; *Diary of a Fly*; *Diary of a Spider*; *Bloom*.

dePaola, Tomie. *Strega Nona*; *The Legend of the Bluebonnet*.

DiCamillo, Kate. Mercy Watson series.

Freeman, Don. *Corduroy*.

Grahame, Kenneth. *The Wind in the Willows*, illustrated by Ernest Shephard (Scribner's, 1959).

Grimm, Brothers. *An Illustrated Treasury of Grimm's Fairy Tales*, illustrated by Daniela Drescher (Floris Books, 2013).

Harris, Joel Chandler. *Uncle Remus*. (While the frame story with the storyteller Uncle Remus is problematic, the Br'er Rabbit stories are a unique contribution to American folklore from the African American tradition.)

Henkes, Kevin. *Lilly's Purple Plastic Purse*; *Julius, the Baby of the World*.

Keats, Ezra Jack. *The Snowy Day*; *John Henry: An American Legend*.

Kellogg, Steven. *Paul Bunyan*; *Pecos Bill*; *The Day Jimmy's Boa Ate the Wash*.

Kipling, Rudyard. *The Jungle Book*.

Lamb, Charles, and Mary Lamb. *Tales from Shakespeare*.

Lang, Andrew. *The Blue Fairy Book*.

Lear, Edward. "The Owl and the Pussy-Cat."

Lobel, Arnold. Frog and Toad series, and any others by him.

Lofting, Hugh. *Doctor Dolittle's Circus*, and others in the series.

Martin, Bill, Jr., and John Archambault. *Chicka Chicka Boom Boom*.

McCaulley, Esau. *Josey Johnson's Hair and the Holy Spirit*, illustrated by LaTonya Jackson (InterVarsity, 2022).

Milne, A. A. *Winnie the Pooh*, and others in the series.

The Original Mother Goose: Based on the 1916 Classic, illustrated by Blanche Fisher Wright (Running Press Kids, 1992).

Polacco, Patricia. *Aunt Chip and the Great Triple Creek Dam Affair*.

Potter, Beatrix. *The Tale of Peter Rabbit* and others.

Dr. Seuss. Any and all of them!

Slobodkina, Esphyr. *Caps for Sale*.

Sorell, Traci. *We Are Grateful: Otsaliheliga*, illustrated by Frané Lessac (Charlesbridge, 2021).

Weatherford, Carole Boston. *Moses: When Harriet Tubman Led Her People to Freedom*.

School Age (Ages 7–12)

Alcott, Louisa May. *Little Women*.

Alexander, Lloyd. *The Black Cauldron*.

Babbitt, Natalie. *Tuck Everlasting*.

Browning, Robert. *The Pied Piper of Hamelin*, illustrated by Kate Greenaway (Pook Press, 2015).

Burnett, Frances Hodgson. *The Secret Garden*.

Butler, Octavia E. *Kindred*, graphic novel adaptation by Damian Duffy and John Jennings (Abrams ComicArts, 2018). (More for ten- to twelve-year-olds.)

Dahl, Roald. *Charlie and the Chocolate Factory*; *Matilda*; *The BFG*, and others.

DiCamillo, Kate. *Flora and Ulysses*; *The Tale of Despereaux*.

Dickens, Charles. *Christmas Carol*; *David Copperfield*; *Oliver Twist* (especially the BBC dramatizations of these novels).

Great Illustrated Classics series.

Juster, Norton. *The Phantom Tollbooth*.

Konigsburg, E. L. *From the Mixed-Up Files of Mrs. Basil E. Frankweiler*; *A Proud Taste for Scarlet and Miniver*.

Latham, Jennifer. *Dreamland Burning*.

L'Engle, Madeleine. *A Wrinkle in Time*.

Lewis, C. S. *Chronicles of Narnia* (Focus on the Family's radio theater editions are great).

Lowry, Lois. *Number the Stars*; *The Giver*.

Montgomery, Lucy Maud. *Anne of Green Gables*.

Nelson, Marilyn. *Carver: A Life in Poems*; *A Wreath for Emmett Till*.

O'Brien, Robert C. *Mrs. Frisby and the Rats of NIMH*.

Paterson, Katherine. *Bridge to Terabithia*; *Parzival*, and all the rest!

Pyle, Howard. *The Merry Adventures of Robin Hood*, and others.

Rogers, Jonathan. The Wilderking Trilogy.

Sachar, Louis. *Holes*; the Wayside School series.

Sewell, Anna. *Black Beauty*.

Smith, S. D. The Green Ember series.

Spyri, Johanna. *Heidi*.

Stevenson, Robert Louis. *Treasure Island*; *Kidnapped*, and others.

Stowe, Harriet Beecher. *Uncle Tom's Cabin*.

Stratford, Jordan. The Wollstonecraft Detective Agency series.

Tolkien, J. R. R. *The Hobbit*.

Twain, Mark. *The Adventures of Tom Sawyer*; *Adventures of Huckleberry Finn*; *The Prince and the Pauper*.

Verne, Jules. *Around the World in Eighty Days*, and many others.

White, E. B. *Charlotte's Web*.

White, T. H. *The Once and Future King*.

Wilder, Laura Ingalls. *Little House on the Prairie*, and others.

Wood, Maryrose. The Incorrigible Children of Ashton Place series.

Wyss, Johann. *The Swiss Family Robinson*.

Yang, Gene Luen. *Boxers & Saints*.

Adolescence (Ages 12–16)

Curtis, Christopher Paul. *Bud, Not Buddy*.

Dickens, Charles. *A Tale of Two Cities*; *Great Expectations*.

Dickinson, Emily. *Collected Poems*.

Doyle, Arthur Conan. Sherlock Holmes series.

Dumas, Alexandre. *The Three Musketeers*, and others.

Du Maurier, Daphne. *Rebecca*.

Eliot, George. *Middlemarch*.

Forbes, Esther. *Johnny Tremain.*

Frank, Anne. *The Diary of a Young Girl.*

Hansberry, Lorraine. *A Raisin in the Sun.*

Hinton, S. E. *The Outsiders.*

Homer. *The Iliad*; *The Odyssey* (Gareth Hinds's graphic novel versions by Candlewick Press are great, and Rosemary Sutcliff's *Black Ships before Troy: The Story of The Iliad* by Delacorte Press [1993] is a good YA version).

Hugo, Victor. *Les Misérables*; *The Hunchback of Notre-Dame.*

Keller, Helen. *The Story of My Life.*

London, Jack. *The Call of the Wild.*

Orwell, George. *Animal Farm.*

Poe, Edgar Allan. *Tales of the Grotesque and Arabesque*, and poems.

Scott, Walter. *Ivanhoe*; *Rob Roy*, and many others.

Shakespeare. *A Midsummer Night's Dream*; *Romeo and Juliet*; *The Merchant of Venice.*

Shelley, Mary. *Frankenstein.*

Swift, Jonathan. *Gulliver's Travels.*

Tolkien, J. R. R. *The Lord of the Rings.*

Walker, Alice. *The Color Purple.*

Wells, H. G. *The Time Machine*; *The Invisible Man*, and others.

White, T. H. *The Sword in the Stone.*

Great Books: The Living Tradition

In no way can this list be comprehensive. It is only meant as a starting place for those interested in reading classics. I did not choose all the works that have been influential, but the "best that has been thought and said" even among writers ignored by their time and place.

Ancient Authors

Aristotle. *Nicomachean Ethics*; *Poetics*; *Rhetoric.* Check out Philip Freeman's translation of *Poetics* titled *How to Tell a Story* (Princeton University Press, 2022).

Beowulf, translated by Seamus Heaney (Norton, 2001).

Cappadocian theologians: Gregory of Nyssa, Basil the Great, Macrina.

Confucius. *Analects*, translated by Annping Chin (Penguin, 2014).

Epic of Gilgamesh, translated by Stephen Mitchell (Atria Books, 2006).

Epictetus. *The Art of Living*, edited by Sharon Lebell (HarperOne, 2007).

Homer. *The Iliad*, translated by Caroline Alexander (Ecco 2016); *The Odyssey*, translated by Emily Wilson (Norton, 2018).

Lao Tzu. *Tao Te Ching*, translated by Ursula K. Le Guin (Shambhala, 2019).

Ovid. *Metamorphoses*, translated by Stanley Lombardo (Hackett, 2010).

Perpetua. *The Passion of Perpetua* (the Latin text with vocabulary and commentary), edited by Mia Donato et al. (Pixelia, 2021). (Great for classical schools.)

Plato. *The Republic; Timaeus; The Trial and Death of Socrates: Four Dialogues.*

Searching for Sappho: The Lost Songs and World of the First Woman Poet, translated by Philip Freeman (Norton, 2016).

Sophocles. Oedipus trilogy, translated by Bryan Doerries (Penguin, 2021).

Virgil. *The Aeneid*, translated by Sarah Ruden (Yale University Press, 2021).

Medieval Authors

The Annotated Arabian Nights: Tales from 1001 Nights, edited by Paulo Lemos Horta, translated by Yasmine Seale (Liveright, 2021).

Aquinas, Thomas. *Summa Theologiae* (for a more accessible version, see Peter Kreeft, *Summa of the Summa* [Ignatius, 1990]).

Augustine. *Confessions*, translated by Sarah Ruden (Modern Library, 2018); *De Doctrina Christiana.*

Boethius. *On the Consolation of Philosophy.*

Chaucer, Geoffrey. *The Canterbury Tales.*

Dante. *The Divine Comedy*, translated by Anthony Esolen (Modern Library, 2003–2007) or Mary Jo Bang (Graywolf, 2013, 2021).

de la Cruz, Sor Juana Inés. *Selected Works*, translated by Edith Grossman, introduction by Julia Alvarez (Norton, 2016).

de Pizan, Christine. *The Book of the City of Ladies.*

Julian of Norwich. *Revelations of Divine Love.*

Kempe, Margery. *The Book of Margery Kempe.*

Marie de France. *Lais of Marie de France.*

Reformers and Counter-Reformers: John Calvin, Desiderius Erasmus, Martin Luther, et al.

Shikibu, Murasaki. *The Tale of Genji*, translated by Dennis Washburn (Norton, 2015).

Teresa of Ávila. *The Interior Castle.*

Early Modern Authors

Austen, Jane. *Pride and Prejudice*, and others.

Bunyan, John. *The Pilgrim's Progress.*

Cervantes, Miguel de. *Don Quixote.*

Dickinson, Emily. *Collected Poems.*

Dostoevsky, Fyodor. *Crime and Punishment*, translated by Oliver Ready (Penguin, 2015); *The Brothers Karamazov*, translated by Richard Pevear and Larissa Volokhonsky (Farrar, Straus and Giroux, 2002).

Douglass, Frederick. All three autobiographies.

Equiano, Olaudah. *The Interesting Narrative of the Life of Olaudah Equiano.*

Goethe, Johann Wolfgang von. *Faust*; *The Sorrows of Young Werther.*

Kierkegaard, Søren. *Fear and Trembling*, and others.

Melville, Herman. *Moby-Dick*; *Benito Cereno*, and others.

Metaphysical poets: John Donne, George Herbert, and others.

Milton, John. *Paradise Lost.*

More, Thomas. *Utopia.*

Nietzsche, Friedrich. *Beyond Good and Evil*, and others.

Romantic poets: Samuel Taylor Coleridge, William Wordsworth, and others.

Shakespeare. *Macbeth*; *As You Like It.*

Transcendentalists: Ralph Waldo Emerson, Henry David Thoreau, and others.

Victorian poets: Alfred Lord Tennyson, Elizabeth Barrett Browning, and others.

Wheatley, Phillis. *Poems on Various Subjects, Religious and Moral.*

Appendix C

Twentieth-Century Authors

Achebe, Chinua. *Things Fall Apart.*
Borges, Jorge Luis. *Collected Fictions.*
Camus, Albert. *The Stranger; The Plague*, and others.
Chekhov, Anton. Stories and plays.
Eliot, T. S. *Four Quartets.*
Ellison, Ralph. *Invisible Man.*
Gaines, Ernest. *A Gathering of Old Men; A Lesson before Dying.*
Harlem poets: Claude McKay, Langston Hughes, Countee Cullen, and others.
Kafka, Franz. *The Metamorphosis; The Trial*, and others.
Márquez, Gabriel García. *One Hundred Years of Solitude.*
Solzhenitsyn, Aleksandr. *The Gulag Archipelago*, and others.
Vonnegut, Kurt. *Slaughterhouse-Five.*

Writers Whose Works Touch the Sacred and the Profane

Beha, Christopher. *The Index of Self-Destructive Acts*, and others.
Bernanos, Georges. *The Diary of a Country Priest.*
Berry, Wendell. *The Sabbath Poems; Hannah Coulter*, and others.
Boyagoda, Randy. *Beggar's Feast*, and others.
Buechner, Frederick. *Godric*, and others.
Cairns, Scott. *Endless Life: Poems of the Mystics.*
Cather, Willa. *My Ántonia; Death Comes for the Archbishop*, and others.
Chesterton, G. K. Father Brown series; *The Everlasting Man; A Man Who Was Thursday.*
Enger, Leif. *Virgil Wander*, and others.
Gioia, Dana. Poetry collections.
Godden, Rumer. *In This House of Brede*, and others.
Hansen, Ron. *Exiles*, and others.
Houselander, Caryll. *The Dry Wood*, and others.
Hurston, Zora Neale. *Moses, Man of the Mountain.*
James, P. D. *The Children of Men.*
Klay, Phil. *Redeployment.*
Lodge, David. *Souls and Bodies.*

174

Lynch, Thomas. Poetry collections.

Manzoni, Alessandro. *The Betrothed.*

Mauriac, François. *The Viper's Tangle,* and others.

Merton, Thomas. *The Seven Storey Mountain,* and others.

Morrison, Toni. *Beloved.*

Nelson, Marilyn. Poetry collections.

O'Brien, Michael. *Father Elijah,* and others.

O'Connor, Flannery. *Collected Works.*

O'Toole, John Kennedy. *A Confederacy of Dunces.*

Percy, Walker. *The Moviegoer,* and others.

Powers, J. F. *Morte d'Urban,* and others.

Quade, Kirstin Valdez. "Christina the Astonishing"; *The Five Wounds.*

Robinson, Marilynne. *Gilead.*

Saunders, George. *Tenth of December.*

Sayers, Dorothy. *Gaudy Night; The Man Born to Be King,* and others.

Spark, Muriel. *Memento Mori; The Prime of Miss Jean Brodie.*

Undset, Sigrid. *Kristin Lavransdatter,* and others.

Vodolazkin, Eugene. *Laurus; Brisbane; The Aviator.*

Wangerin, Walter, Jr. *The Book of the Dun Cow,* and others.

Wiman, Christian. *My Bright Abyss,* and poetry collections.

Notes

Chapter 1 What Kind of Reader Are You?

1. Franz Kafka, letter to Oskar Pollak, January 27, 1904, in *Letters to Friends, Family, and Editors* (New York: Knopf, 2013).

2. Drawn from Flannery O'Connor, "Novelist and Believer," in *Mystery and Manners: Occasional Prose*, ed. Sally Fitzgerald and Robert Fitzgerald (New York: Farrar, Straus and Giroux, 1969), 154–68.

3. C. S. Lewis, "Christianity and Culture," in *Christian Reflections* (Grand Rapids: Eerdmans, 1967), 42.

4. Thomas Jefferson, letter to John Adams, June 10, 1815, https://www.loc.gov/exhibits/jefferson/217.html.

5. George Herbert, "Jordan (II)," in *The English Poems of George Herbert*, ed. C. A. Patrides (London: J. M. Dent & Sons, 1974), 116–17, available at http://www.luminarium.org/sevenlit/herbert/jordan2.htm.

6. J. R. R. Tolkien, "On Fairy-Stories," in *The Monsters and the Critics and Other Essays*, ed. Christopher Tolkien (New York: HarperCollins, 1997), 148.

7. T. S. Eliot, "Tradition and the Individual Talent," originally published 1919, available at https://www.poetryfoundation.org/articles/69400/tradition-and-the-individual-talent.

8. Frederick Douglass, *The Life and Times of Frederick Douglass* (Boston: De Wolfe & Fiske, 1892).

9. United States George Washington Bicentennial Commission, *George Washington: The Man of Action in Military and Civil Life* (Washington, DC: US Government Printing Office, 1931), 11.

10. Peter Manseau, *The Jefferson Bible: A Biography* (Princeton: Princeton University Press, 2020), 5.

11. "I never go to bed without an hour, or half hour's previous reading of something moral, whereon to ruminate in the intervals of sleep." Thomas

Jefferson, letter to Vine Utley, March 21, 1819, in *The Papers of Thomas Jefferson*, ed. J. Jefferson Looney (Princeton: Princeton University Press, 2004), 14:156–58.

12. "Thus a lively and lasting sense of filial duty is more effectually impressed on the mind of a son or daughter by reading King Lear, than by all the dry volumes of ethics and divinity that ever were written." Thomas Jefferson, letter to Robert Skipwith, August 3, 1771, National Archives, Founders Online, https://founders.archives.gov/documents/Jefferson/01-01-02-0056.

13. Jefferson, letter to Skipwith, August 3, 1771.

14. Manseau, *Jefferson Bible*, 5.

15. Manseau, *Jefferson Bible*, 8.

16. Manseau, *Jefferson Bible*, 8.

17. George H. Nash, *Books and the Founding Fathers* (Wilmington, DE: ISI Books, 2008), 14.

18. C. S. Lewis, *Studies in Medieval and Renaissance Literature*, Canto Classics (Cambridge: Cambridge University Press, 1998), 2–3.

19. George Steiner, "'Critic'/'Reader,'" in *George Steiner: A Reader* (New York: Oxford University Press, 1984), 94–95.

20. David Lyle Jeffrey explains, "Considered philologically, the reader is one who finally '*understands*' (*sub stantia*). Thus he 'stands under' an *auctoritas*, most often regarded as a 'who.' The reader wants to know this 'who.'" Jeffrey, *Houses of the Interpreter: Reading Scripture, Reading Culture* (Waco: Baylor University Press, 2009), 181.

21. William F. Lynch, *Christ and Apollo: The Dimensions of the Literary Imagination* (Wilmington, DE: ISI Books, 2004), 256.

22. There is much debate about what constitutes literacy in the ancient world, and scholars go back and forth about whether there was widespread and dense literacy in the Roman Empire. "The composition, circulation, and use of Christian writings in the early church are manifest proof of Christian literacy but say nothing in themselves about the extent of literacy within Christianity." Harry Gamble, *Books and Readers in the Early Church: A History of Early Christian Texts* (New Haven: Yale University Press, 1995), 4.

23. David Lyle Jeffrey chronicles our Christian reverence for books in *People of the Book: Christian Identity and Literary Culture* (Grand Rapids: Eerdmans, 1996), outlining the connections between "Christian identity and literary culture," as the subtitle relays. We cannot limit reading to mean an individual with a book in her hands who goes over the words silently. More accurately, for hundreds of years, "reading" included passing down books by memory. The educated learned by heart what they read.

24. Ivan Illich argues in *In the Vineyard of the Text: A Commentary to Hugh's "Didascalicon"* (Chicago: University of Chicago Press, 1996) that the move from monastery to scholastic communities of learning made reading "an individualistic activity" (82), and the text became "scrutable" (95) rather than loved. He writes, "A new reader comes into existence, one who wants to acquire in a few years of study a new kind of acquaintance with a larger number of authors than a meditating monk could have perused in a lifetime" (96).

25. Brad S. Gregory, *The Unintended Reformation: How a Religious Revolution Secularized Society* (Cambridge, MA: Belknap, 2012).

26. Augustine, *On Christian Teaching*, preface.7, trans. R. P. H. Green, Oxford World's Classics (Oxford: Oxford University Press, 1997), 4.

27. Valentine Cunningham, *Reading after Theory*, Blackwell Manifestos (Oxford: Blackwell, 2002), 3.

28. "The Library of Babel," in *Collected Fictions: Jorge Luis Borges*, trans. Andrew Hurley (New York: Penguin, 1998), 112.

29. This analysis of Majmudar's poem was first published by the James Martin Center, adapted from a talk I gave at the Word on Fire conference in Orlando, Florida, November 5, 2021.

30. C. S. Lewis, *An Experiment in Criticism* (Cambridge: Cambridge University Press, 1961), 141.

Chapter 2 Why Read Anything but the Bible?

1. Augustine, *On Christian Teaching* 2.27.41, trans. R. P. H. Green, Oxford World's Classics (Oxford: Oxford University Press, 1997), 54.

2. Augustine, *On Christian Teaching* 2.18.28 (Green, 47).

3. Augustine, *On Christian Teaching* 2.40.60–61 (Green, 64–65).

4. Basil of Caesarea, *To Young Men, on How They Might Derive Profit from Pagan Literature*, in *The Great Tradition: Classic Readings on What It Means to Be an Educated Human Being*, ed. Richard M. Gamble (Wilmington, DE: ISI Books, 2007), 183.

5. Basil, *To Young Men*, 183.

6. Basil, *To Young Men*, 183.

7. Basil, *To Young Men*, 184.

8. Basil, *To Young Men*, 188.

9. Horace, *Ars Poetica*, lines 333–65, trans. A. S. Kline, available at Poetry in Translation, 2005, https://www.poetryintranslation.com/PITBR/Latin/HoraceArsPoetica.php.

10. Philip Melanchthon, *Preface to Homer*, in Gamble, *The Great Tradition*, 420.

11. Melanchthon, *Preface to Homer*, 427.

12. Jean Leclercq, *The Love of Learning and the Desire for God: A Study of Monastic Culture*, trans. Catharine Misrahi (New York: Fordham University Press, 1961), 170–71.

13. C. S. Lewis, *An Experiment in Criticism* (Cambridge: Cambridge University Press, 1961), 131–32.

14. Lewis, *Experiment in Criticism*, 132.

15. Søren Kierkegaard, "Of the Difference Between a Genius and an Apostle," 1847, available at https://www.holybooks.com/wp-content/uploads/Of-the-Difference-Between-a-Genius-and-an-Apostle.pdf, 91.

16. Kierkegaard, "Of the Difference," 97 (slightly altered).

17. Kierkegaard, "Of the Difference," 107.

Bookmark 1 Reading like Augustine of Hippo

1. G. K. Chesterton, *Orthodoxy* (Mineola, NY: Dover, 2004), 50.

2. Peter Brown, *Augustine of Hippo: A Biography*, 2nd ed. (Berkeley: University of California Press, 2000), 86.

3. Brian Stock, *Augustine the Reader: Meditation, Self-Knowledge, and the Ethics of Interpretation* (Cambridge, MA: Harvard University Press, 1998), 29–30.

4. Plenty of scholars disagree with this reading of Augustine. Those same people probably take Socrates at his word when he throws out the poets from the republic. Yet why did Socrates turn to drafting verses in the final days of his life (*Phaedo*)? Why did Augustine imitate the *Aeneid*?

5. Augustine, *Confessions* 2.25.22–29, quoted in Stock, *Augustine the Reader*, 202.

6. Camille Bennett, "The Conversion of Vergil: *The Aeneid* in Augustine's *Confessions*," *Revue des Études Augustiniennes* 34 (1988): 64.

7. Augustine, *Confessions* 6.3.3, trans. Henry Chadwick (Oxford: Oxford University Press, 1992), 92–93.

8. Augustine, *Confessions* 3.7.12 (Chadwick, 43).

9. Augustine, *Confessions* 3.7.12 (Chadwick, 43).

10. Augustine, *Confessions* 5.14.24 (Chadwick, 88).

11. Origen, *Commentary on the Canticle of Canticles* 3.12, in *Song of Songs: Commentary and Homilies*, trans. R. P. Lawson, Ancient Christian Writers 26 (New York: Newman, 1957), 218.

12. Augustine, *The Literal Meaning of Genesis* 1.1.1, in *On Genesis*, trans. Edmund Hill, The Works of St. Augustine: A Translation for the 21st Century I/13 (Hyde Park, NY: New City Press, 2002), 168.

13. Augustine, *On Christian Teaching* 2.9.14, trans. R. P. H. Green (Oxford: Oxford University Press, 1997), 37.

14. Brown, *Augustine of Hippo*, 228.

15. Augustine, *On Christian Doctrine* 2.6, trans. D. W. Robertson Jr. (Indianapolis: Bobbs-Merrill, 1977), 32.

16. Flannery O'Connor, "Letters," in *The Collected Works*, ed. Sally Fitzgerald (New York: Library of America, 1988), 1110–11.

17. Augustine, *On Christian Doctrine* 2.6.8 (Robertson, 38).

18. Augustine, *On Christian Doctrine* 2.6.8 (Robertson, 38).

19. Mary Carruthers, *The Craft of Thought: Meditation, Rhetoric, and the Making of Images, 400–1200* (Cambridge: Cambridge University Press, 2000), 124.

20. Hans Boersma, *Scripture as Real Presence: Sacramental Exegesis in the Early Church* (Grand Rapids: Baker Academic, 2017), 47.

21. Augustine, *Confessions* 12.18.27 (Chadwick, 259).

22. Augustine, *On Christian Teaching* 1.36.40 (Green, 27).

23. This insight comes from David Lyle Jeffrey.

24. John Calvin, *Institutes of the Christian Religion* 1.1.1, trans. Henry Beveridge (Grand Rapids: Eerdmans, 1989), Christian Classics Ethereal Library, https://www.ccel.org/ccel/calvin/institutes.iii.ii.html.

25. Susan Sontag, "Susan Sontag: A Letter to Borges," letter dated June 13, 1996, *Independent*, January 24, 2002, https://www.independent.co.uk/arts -entertainment/books/features/susan-sontag-a-letter-to-borges-9158988.html.

26. Flannery O'Connor, *A Prayer Journal*, ed. William A. Sessions (New York: Farrar, Straus & Giroux, 2013), 4.

27. Gerard Manley Hopkins, "As Kingfishers Catch Fire," in *Gerard Manley Hopkins: Poems and Prose* (New York: Penguin Classics, 1985), available at https://www.poetryfoundation.org/poems/44389/as-kingfishers-catch-fire.

28. Flannery O'Connor, "On Her Own Work," in *Mystery and Manners: Occasional Prose*, ed. Sally Fitzgerald and Robert Fitzgerald (New York: Farrar, Straus & Giroux, 1969), 108.

29. Tim Parks, "A Weapon for Readers," *New York Review of Books*, December 3, 2014, https://www.nybooks.com/daily/2014/12/03/weapon-for-readers.

30. Mortimer Adler and Charles Van Doren, *How to Read a Book: The Classic Guide to Intelligent Reading*, rev. ed. (New York: Touchstone, 2014), 49.

31. Billy Collins, "Marginalia," *Poetry* (February 1996): 250, available at https://www.poetryfoundation.org/poetrymagazine/browse?contentId=39493.

32. Italo Calvino, *Why Read the Classics?*, trans. Martin McLaughlin (New York: Mariner Books, 1991), 5.

33. Collins, "Marginalia."

34. Although William V. Harris, in *Ancient Literacy* (Cambridge, MA: Harvard University Press, 1991), argues that no more than 10 percent of the Roman world were literate, Harry Gamble's *Books and Readers in the Early Church: A History of Early Christian Texts* (New Haven: Yale University Press, 1995) evidences how the early church promoted a literary culture that prevailed in spite of a narrow definition of literacy. See also Larry W. Hurtado's *Destroyer of the gods: Early Christian Distinctiveness in the Roman World* (Waco: Baylor University Press, 2016), 105–41. On Luther and Bible translation, see David Morgan, "A Brief History of Bible Translation," Wycliffe Bible Translators, https://www.wycliffe.org.uk/stories/a-brief-history-of-bible-translation.

35. Palladius, *The Lausiac History*, trans. R. T. Meyer, Ancient Christian Writers 34 (New York: Paulist Press, 1964), 137.

36. Gerontius, *The Life of Holy Melania*, in *Handmaids of the Lord: Contemporary Descriptions of Feminine Asceticism in the First Six Christian Centuries*, trans. Joan Peterson, Cistercian Studies (Kalamazoo, MI: Cistercian Publications, 1996), 327.

Chapter 3 What's the Difference between "Use" and "Enjoy"?

1. Augustine, *On Christian Teaching* 1.2.3, trans. R. P. H. Green (Oxford: Oxford University Press, 1997), 9.

2. Augustine, *On Christian Teaching* 1.3.3 (Green, 9).

3. Diane Glancy, *A Line of Driftwood: The Ada Blackjack Story* (New York: Turtle Point Press, 2021), 17.

4. John Keats, "Ode on a Grecian Urn," Poetry Foundation, accessed August 19, 2022, https://www.poetryfoundation.org/poems/44477/ode-on-a-grecian -urn.

5. Sections of this chapter were originally published as Jessica Hooten Wilson, "In Praise of Useless Reading," *The Gospel Coalition*, January 25, 2019, https://www.thegospelcoalition.org/article/praise-useless-reading.

6. Vigen Guroian, "Why Should Businessmen Read Great Literature?," *Religion & Liberty* 12, no. 4 (July 20, 2010), https://www.acton.org/pub/religion -liberty/volume-12-number-4/why-should-businessmen-read-great-literature.

7. Thomas Lynch, "Heavenward," in *Still Life in Milford* (New York: Norton, 1998), 100.

8. C. S. Lewis, *The Abolition of Man* (New York: HarperOne, 2015), 25.

9. John Stuart Mill, *Autobiography* (1873; repr., New York: Columbia University Press, 1960), 104.

10. Alan Jacobs, *How to Think: A Survival Guide for a World at Odds* (New York: Currency, 2017), 44.

11. Flannery O'Connor, *A Prayer Journal*, ed. William A. Sessions (New York: Farrar, Straus & Giroux, 2013), 34.

12. Flanner O'Connor, "Novelist and Believer," in *Mystery and Manners: Occasional Prose*, ed. Sally Fitzgerald and Robert Fitzgerald (New York: Farrar, Straus & Giroux, 1969), 168.

13. Flannery O'Connor, "Revelation," in *Collected Works* (New York: Library of America, 1988), 653.

14. Gerard Manley Hopkins, "As Kingfishers Catch Fire," in *Gerard Manley Hopkins: Poems and Prose* (New York: Penguin Classics, 1985), available at https://www.poetryfoundation.org/poems/44389/as-kingfishers-catch-fire.

15. Gerard Manley Hopkins, "Hurrahing in Harvest," available at https:// www.bartleby.com/122/14.html.

16. Sections of this chapter were published originally as Jessica Hooten Wilson, "All This Useless Beauty," *Church Life Journal*, January 21, 2020, https:// churchlifejournal.nd.edu/articles/all-this-useless-beauty.

17. Westminster Shorter Catechism, question 1, available at https://www .apuritansmind.com/westminster-standards/shorter-catechism.

18. C. S. Lewis, *An Experiment in Criticism* (Cambridge: Cambridge University Press, 1961), 19.

19. Lewis, *Experiment in Criticism*, 32.

20. Lewis, *Experiment in Criticism*, 19.

21. Simone Weil, "Reflections on the Right Use of School Studies with a View to the Love of God," in *Waiting on God*, trans. Emma Crauford (London: Fontana Books, 1959), 114.

22. Sarah Bro Trasmundi and Stephen J. Cowley, "Reading: How Readers Beget Imagining," *Frontiers in Psychology*, September 24, 2020, https://doi.org /10.3389/fpsyg.2020.531682.

Chapter 4 Do Good Books Make You a Good Person?

1. Marie de France, *The Lais of Marie de France*, trans. Glyn S. Burgess and Keith Busby (New York: Penguin, 1986), 41.

2. Leonardo Bruni, *On the Study of Literature*, in *The Great Tradition: Classic Readings on What It Means to Be an Educated Human Being*, ed. Richard M. Gamble (Wilmington, DE: ISI Books, 2007), 333.

3. Quoted by Jennifer D. Webb, the oration of Ludovico Carbone (1430–85), "Hidden in Plain Sight: Varano and Sforza Women of the Marche," in *Wives, Widows, Mistresses, and Nuns in Early Modern Italy: Making the Invisible Visible through Art and Patronage*, ed. Katherine A. McIver (New York: Routledge, 2016), 13.

4. Harold Bloom, "The Necessity of Misreading," *The Georgia Review* 29, no. 2 (Summer 1975): 269, http://www.jstor.org/stable/41397178.

5. Bloom, "Necessity of Misreading," 285.

6. Dante, *Paradiso*, canto 17, line 118, available at http://www.worldofdante .org/comedy/dante/paradise.xml/3.17.

7. Mortimer Adler and Charles Van Doren, *How to Read a Book: The Classic Guide to Intelligent Reading*, rev. ed. (New York: Touchstone, 2014), 45.

8. David Mikics, *Slow Reading in a Hurried Age* (Cambridge, MA: Belknap, 2013).

9. Georges Bernanos, *The Diary of a Country Priest* (New York: Image, 1954), 232.

10. Hans Boersma, *Scripture as Real Presence: Sacramental Exegesis in the Early Church* (Grand Rapids: Baker Academic, 2017), 263.

Bookmark 2 Reading like Julian of Norwich

1. Julia Bolton Holloway, *Julian among the Books: Julian of Norwich's Theological Library* (Newcastle upon Tyne: Cambridge Scholars, 2016), xii.

2. Holloway writes, "In all these versions [of *Revelations of Divine Love*], except the last, Julian gives copious passages from the Bible in her Middle English, from Genesis, from Exodus, from the Psalms, from Isaiah, from Jonah, from the Epistles, and much else, but she dares not do so in the 1413 version when to own or use John Wyclif's translation of the Bible into English would have caused one to have been burnt at the stake in chains as a Lollard heretic." *Julian among the Books*, 6.

3. Margery Kempe writes of visiting "Dame Julian" in her autobiography: "Great was the holy conversation that the anchoress and this creature had through talking of the love of our Lord Jesus Christ for the many days that they were together." *Medieval Writings on Female Spirituality*, ed. Elizabeth Spearing (New York: Penguin, 2022), 231.

4. *Ancrene Wisse: Guide for Anchoresses*, trans. Hugh White (New York: Penguin, 1994).

5. Marie de France, *The Lais of Marie de France*, trans. Glyn S. Burgess and Keith Busby (New York: Penguin, 1986), 41.

6. Brian FitzGerald, "Prophecy and the Contemplation of History: Peter John Olivi and Hugh of St. Victor," in *Exploring Lost Dimensions in Christian Mysticism: Opening to the Mystical*, ed. Louise Nelstrop and Simon D. Podmore (New York: Ashgate, 2013), 184.

7. Denys Turner, *Julian of Norwich, Theologian* (New Haven: Yale University Press, 2011), 79.

8. Julian of Norwich, *Revelations of Divine Love* 5, Long Text (hereafter LT), trans. Elizabeth Spearing (New York: Penguin, 1998), 47.

9. Phil Vischer, Christian Taylor, and Skye Jethani, "Episode 507: Dubuque, Demons, & Defying Patriarchy (Part Deux) with Beth Allison Barr," *Holy Post* (podcast), May 4, 2022, https://www.holypost.com/post/episode-507-dubuque -demons-defying-patriarchy-part-deux-with-beth-allison-barr.

10. Ryan McDermott, *Tropologies: Ethics and Invention in England, c. 1350– 1600*, ReFormations: Medieval and Early Modern (Notre Dame, IN: University of Notre Dame Press, 2016), 27.

11. Julian, *Revelations of Divine Love* 9, LT (Spearing, 53).

12. Barbara Newman, *The Permeable Self: Five Medieval Relationships*, Middle Ages Series (Philadelphia: University of Pennsylvania Press, 2021), 264.

13. Julian, *Revelations of Divine Love* 25, LT (Spearing, 77).

14. Holloway, *Julian among the Books*, 79.

15. Donyelle C. McCray, *The Censored Pulpit: Julian of Norwich as Preacher* (Minneapolis: Fortress, 2019), 7.

16. Julian, *Revelations of Divine Love* 57, LT (Spearing, 136).

17. Julian of Norwich, *Revelations of Divine Love* 57, LT, trans. Grace Warrack (Grand Rapids: Christian Classics Ethereal Library, 2002), 138, https:// ccel.org/ccel/julian/revelations/revelations.xvi.xiv.html.

18. McCray, *Censored Pulpit*, 20.

19. David Lyle Jeffrey, *People of the Book: Christian Identity and Literary Culture* (Grand Rapids: Eerdmans, 1996), 381.

20. McDermott, *Tropologies*, 12.

21. Julian, *Revelations of Divine Love* 86, LT (Spearing, 179).

22. Augustine, *Confessions* 12.18.27 (Chadwick, 259).

23. Julian, *Revelations of Divine Love* 86, LT (Spearing, 179).

24. Julian, *Revelations of Divine Love* 26, 30, LT (Spearing, 78, 82).

25. E.g., Hrotsvitha, Marguerite Porete, Marie de France, Christine de Pizan, Margery Kempe, Hildegard von Bingen, Birgitta of Sweden, Catherine of Siena, Mechthild of Magdeburg, Marguerite de Navarre, Elisabeth of Schönau, Anna Komnene, Trota of Salerno, Laura Cereta, and so on.

26. Dorothy L. Sayers, "Are Women Human?," in *A Matter of Eternity: Selections from the Writings of Dorothy L. Sayers*, ed. Rosamond Kent Sprague (Grand Rapids: Eerdmans, 1973), 46–47.

27. Laura Saetveit Miles, *The Virgin Mary's Book at Annunciation* (Cambridge: Brewer, 2020), 3.

28. Miles, *Virgin Mary's Book at Annunciation*, 4.

29. Sayers, "Are Women Human?," 47.

30. Julian, *Revelations of Divine Love* 6, Short Text (hereafter ST) (Spearing, 11).

31. Quoted in A. C. Spearing, introduction to Julian of Norwich, *Revelations of Divine Love*, xvii.

32. Julian, *Revelations of Divine Love* 6, ST (Spearing, 11).

Chapter 5 What Does the Trinity Have to Do with the ART of Reading?

1. Stanley Fish, *Is There a Text in This Class? The Authority of Interpretive Communities* (Cambridge, MA: Harvard University Press, 1982).

2. Stephen Prickett, *Words and the Word: Language, Poetics and Biblical Interpretation* (Cambridge: Cambridge University Press, 1988), 189. Prickett was a student of C. S. Lewis.

3. Makoto Fujimura, *Art and Faith: A Theology of Making* (New Haven: Yale University Press, 2021), 75.

4. Fujimura, *Art and Faith*, 76.

5. Dorothy Sayers, *The Mind of the Maker* (New York: HarperOne, 1987), 37–38:

> For every work of creation is threefold, an earthly trinity to match the heavenly. First, there is the Creative Idea, passionless, timeless, beholding the whole work complete at once, the end in the beginning: and this is the image of the Father.
>
> Second, there is the Creative Energy begotten of that idea, working in time from the beginning to the end, with sweat and passion, being incarnate in the bond of matter, and this is the image of the Word.
>
> Third there is the Creative Power, the meaning of the work and its response in the lively soul: and this is the image of the indwelling Spirit.
>
> And these three are one, each equally in itself the whole work, whereof none can exist without the other: and this is the image of the Trinity.

6. Flannery O'Connor, "Some Aspects of the Grotesque in Southern Fiction," in *The Collected Works*, ed. Sally Fitzgerald (New York: Library of America, 1988), 817.

7. O'Connor, "Some Aspects," 804.

8. Louis Markos, *From Achilles to Christ: Why Christians Should Read the Pagan Classics* (Downers Grove, IL: IVP Academic, 2007), 13.

9. Fyodor Dostoevsky, *The Brothers Karamazov*, trans. Richard Pevear and Larissa Volokhonsky (New York: Farrar, Straus & Giroux, 1990), 260.

10. Hans Boersma, *Scripture as Real Presence: Sacramental Exegesis in the Early Church* (Grand Rapids: Baker Academic, 2017), 12.

11. John J. O'Keefe and R. R. Reno, *Sanctified Vision: An Introduction to Early Christian Interpretation of the Bible* (Baltimore: Johns Hopkins University Press, 2005), 41.

12. Maria Skobtsova, *Mother Maria Skobtsova: Essential Writings* (New York: Orbis Books, 2002), 57.

13. Dante, *Paradiso* 1.1.1–3, https://digitaldante.columbia.edu/dante/divine-comedy/paradiso/paradiso-1.

14. Flanner O'Connor, "Some Aspects of the Grotesque in Southern Fiction," in *Mystery and Manners: Occasional Prose*, ed. Sally Fitzgerald and Robert Fitzgerald (New York: Farrar, Straus & Giroux, 1969), 44.

15. Alan Jacobs, *A Theology of Reading: The Hermeneutics of Love* (Boulder, CO: Westview, 2001), 145.

16. Jacobs, *Theology of Reading*, 145.

Bookmark 3 Reading like Frederick Douglass

1. Frederick Douglass, *My Bondage and My Freedom* (New York: Penguin, 2003), 109.

2. Frederick Douglass, *The Life and Times of Frederick Douglass* (Boston: De Wolfe & Fiske, 1892), 247.

3. David Blight, *Frederick Douglass: Prophet of Freedom* (New York: Simon & Schuster, 2018), 44.

4. Douglass, *My Bondage and My Freedom*, 158.

5. Quoted in Eric Ashley Hairston, *The Ebony Column: Classics, Civilization, and the African American Reclamation of the West* (Knoxville: University of Tennessee Press, 2016), 100–101.

6. Hairston, *Ebony Column*, 87.

7. Douglass, *My Bondage and My Freedom*, 101 and 68, respectively.

8. Blight, *Frederick Douglass*, 28.

9. Blight, *Frederick Douglass*, 515.

10. Ludwig Feuerbach, *Lectures on the Essence of Religion*, trans. Ralph Manheim (repr., Eugene, OR: Wipf & Stock, 2018), 187.

11. Blight, *Frederick Douglass*, 516.

12. Frederick Douglass, appendix to *Life of an American Slave* (Boston: Anti-Slavery Office, 1845), 120.

13. Adam Gopnik, "The Prophetic Pragmatism of Frederick Douglass," *New Yorker*, October 8, 2018, https://www.newyorker.com/magazine/2018/10/15/the-prophetic-pragmatism-of-frederick-douglass.

14. Frederick Douglass, speech at the thirty-third anniversary of the Jerry Rescue, Syracuse, New York, 1884, Frederick Douglass Papers (Library of Congress).

15. Letter to Mr. A. C. C. Thompson of Delaware, January 27, 1846, which appears as an appendix to the 2nd Dublin edition of *Narrative of the Life of Frederick Douglass, an American Slave* (Dublin: Webb and Chapman, 1846).

16. W. E. B. Du Bois, *The Souls of Black Folk* (Brooklyn, NY: Restless Books, 2017), 103.

17. Anna Julia Cooper, *The Voice of Anna Julia Cooper*, ed. Charles Lemert and Esme Bhan (Lanham, MD: Rowan & Littlefield, 1998), 82.

18. James Baldwin, *Conversations with James Baldwin*, ed. Fred L. Standley and Louis H. Pratt (Jackson: University Press of Mississippi, 1989), 143–46.

19. Baldwin, *Conversations with James Baldwin*, 21.

20. Margaret Mead and James Baldwin, *A Rap on Race: From Two of the Twentieth Century's Most Influential Americans* (Philadelphia: Lippincott, 1971), 78.

21. Ray Bradbury, *Fahrenheit 451* (New York: Simon & Schuster, 2012), 83.

22. Bradbury, *Fahrenheit 451*, 58.

23. American Academy of Arts and Sciences, "Time Spent Reading," accessed September 12, 2022, available at https://www.amacad.org/humanities-indicators/public-life/time-spent-reading; "Average Daily Time Spent Reading per Capita in the United States from 2018 to 2020, by Age Group," Statista, July 2021, https://www.statista.com/statistics/412454/average-daily-time-reading-us-by-age.

24. Bradbury, *Fahrenheit 451*, 10.

Chapter 6 Why Do You Need Four Senses to Read?

1. Stephen Prickett, *Words and the Word: Language, Poetics and Biblical Interpretation* (Cambridge: Cambridge University Press, 1988), 217.

2. Eugene Peterson, *Eat This Book: A Conversation in the Art of Spiritual Reading* (Grand Rapids: Eerdmans, 2009), 113.

3. Lucian López describes it as such in "Allegory and Authority: An Exegetical Analysis of Matthew 13," *Obsculta* 10, no. 1 (May 17, 2017): 146.

4. David Lyle Jeffrey, *Houses of the Interpreter: Reading Scripture, Reading Culture* (Waco: Baylor University Press, 2009), 10.

5. John Cassian, *Collatio* 14.8 (Patrologia Latina 49:962–65), trans. William F. Lynch, in the supplements of Lynch, *Christ and Apollo: The Dimensions of the Literary Imagination* (Wilmington, DE: ISI Books, 2004), 305.

6. See Guigo II, *The Ladder of Monks*, in *"The Ladder of Monks: A Letter on the Contemplative Life" and "Twelve Meditations,"* trans. Edmund Colledge and James Walsh, Cistercian Studies (Kalamazoo, MI: Cistercian Publications, 1978), 67–86.

7. Translation by Robert Alter, *The Hebrew Bible: A Translation with Commentary*, vol. 1 (New York: Norton, 2019), at Gen. 28:12

8. Flannery O'Connor, "Church and Fiction Writer," in *Mystery and Manners: Occasional Prose*, ed. Sally Fitzgerald and Robert Fitzgerald (New York: Farrar, Straus & Giroux, 1969), 151.

9. Peterson, *Eat This Book*, 81.

10. Guigo, *Ladder of Monks* (Colledge and Walsh, 68).

11. See Mary Carruthers, *The Craft of Thought: Meditation, Rhetoric, and the Making of Images, 400–1200* (Cambridge: Cambridge University Press, 2000), 136: "The manner in which ancient texts were written out, without word divisions, reinforces this mental habit [constructing], for a reader had to analyze the syllables first before they could be 'glued' together in semantic units."

12. Ivan Illich, *In the Vineyard of the Text: A Commentary to Hugh's "Didascalicon"* (Chicago: University of Chicago Press, 1996), 57. Illich notes how

187

monasteries were described as places of "mumblers and munchers" because they ruminated or chewed on words aloud. He lists a handful of witnesses to this practice (54–55).

13. Jean Leclercq, *The Love of Learning and the Desire for God: A Study of Monastic Culture*, trans. Catharine Misrahi (New York: Fordham University Press, 1961), 90.

14. Peterson, *Eat This Book*, 18.

15. George Herbert, "Love III," in *George Herbert and the Seventeenth-Century Religious Poets*, ed. Mario A. Di Cesare (New York: Norton, 1978), available at Poetry Foundation, https://www.poetryfoundation.org/poems /44367/love-iii.

16. George Herbert, "Easter Wings," Poetry Foundation, https://www.poetry foundation.org/poems/44361/easter-wings.

17. George Herbert, "The Windows," Poetry Foundation, https://www.poetry foundation.org/poems/50695/the-windows-56d22df68ff95.

18. Jordan K. Monson, "My Boss Is a Jewish Construction Worker," *Christianity Today*, November 22, 2021, https://www.christianitytoday.com/ct/2021 /december/jewish-construction-worker-jesus-vocation-profession-stone.html.

19. Lewis Carroll, "Jabberwocky," in *The Random House Book of Poetry for Children* (New York: Random House, 1983), available at Poetry Foundation, https://www.poetryfoundation.org/poems/42916/jabberwocky.

20. Dorothy L. Sayers, "The Fourfold Interpretation of the *Comedy*," in *Introductory Papers on Dante* (London: Methuen, 1954), 103.

21. Hugh of St. Victor, *Didascalicon*, trans. Jerome Taylor (New York: Aeterna, 2020), 119.

22. Flannery O'Connor, "On Her Own Work," in *Mystery and Manners: Occasional Prose*, ed. Sally Fitzgerald and Robert Fitzgerald (New York: Farrar, Straus & Giroux, 1969), 108.

23. O'Connor, "On Her Own Work," 108.

24. Leclercq, *Love of Learning*, 89.

25. James K. A. Smith, *You Are What You Love: The Spiritual Power of Habit* (Grand Rapids: Brazos, 2016), 2.

26. Quoted by Josef Pieper, *Leisure: The Basis of Culture*, trans. Alexander Dru (1963; repr., San Francisco: Ignatius, 2009), 34.

27. Gregory the Great, *Homilies on the Book of Ezekiel*, in *The Great Tradition: Classic Readings on What It Means to Be an Educated Human Being*, ed. Richard M. Gamble (Wilmington, DE: ISI Books, 2007), 238.

28. John J. O'Keefe and R. R. Reno, *Sanctified Vision: An Introduction to Early Christian Interpretation of the Bible* (Baltimore: Johns Hopkins University Press, 2005), 67.

29. The following is taken from a talk I gave at the Higher Ed Summit, which was published as "Cormac McCarthy, Cultural Memory, and the Mythopoesis of Fire," *Church Life Journal*, October 28, 2021, https://churchlifejournal.nd .edu/articles/cormac-mccarthy-cultural-memory-and-the-mythopoesis-of -fire.

30. "He gave you not only his blood but fire as well, for it was through the fire of love that he gave you his blood." Catherine of Siena, *The Dialogue*, trans. Suzanne Noffke (New York: Paulist Press, 1980), 247.

31. Dante, *Purgatorio* 21.95, trans. Robert Hollander, Princeton Dante Project, 1997–1998, https://dante.princeton.edu/dante/pdp/commedia.html.

32. See Aeschylus's play *Prometheus Bound*; in Percy Shelley's play about Prometheus (also called *Prometheus Unbound*), the titan who delivers fire to humans, he writes of truth ever burning like a flame.

33. Cormac McCarthy, *The Road* (New York: Knopf, 2006), 4.

34. Dorothy L. Sayers, "Poetry, Language and Ambiguity," in *The Poetry of Search and the Poetry of Statement* (1963; repr., Eugene, OR: Wipf & Stock, 2006), 272.

35. Martin Luther, Luther's Works, vol. 54, *Table Talk*, ed. and trans. Theodore G. Tappert (Philadelphia: Fortress, 1967), no. 1654.

36. Luther, *Table Talk*, 46–47.

37. Peterson, *Eat This Book*, 102.

38. Peterson, *Eat This Book*, 99.

39. C. S. Lewis, preface to *Perelandra* (New York: Scribner Classics, 1996), 7.

40. J. R. R. Tolkien, foreword to *The Fellowship of the Ring*, 2nd ed. (New York: Houghton Mifflin, 1967), 7.

41. Tolkien, foreword to *The Fellowship of the Ring*, 7.

42. Dorothy L. Sayers, "The Writing and Reading of Allegory," in *The Poetry of Search*, 202.

43. Sayers, "Writing and Reading of Allegory," 216.

44. Gerard Manley Hopkins, "God's Grandeur," in *Gerard Manley Hopkins: Poems and Prose* (New York: Penguin Classics, 1985), available at Poetry Foundation, https://www.poetryfoundation.org/poems/44395/gods-grandeur.

45. John J. Parsons elaborates on all these meanings of Hebrew letters in "The Letter Yod," Hebrew for Christians, https://www.hebrew4christians.com/Grammar/Unit_One/Aleph-Bet/Yod/yod.html.

46. Julia Bolton Holloway, *Julian among the Books: Julian of Norwich's Theological Library* (Newcastle upon Tyne: Cambridge Scholars, 2016), 55.

47. Augustine, *On Christian Teaching* 2.16.23–24, 59, trans. R. P. H. Green (Oxford: Oxford University Press, 1997), 44. Augustine unpacks the figurative meaning of "serpent," then says, "ignorance of other animals . . . is a very great drawback for the reader." He continues to explain that lack of knowledge of plants and numbers will limit a reader's understanding of the Bible (*On Christian Teaching* 2.16.24, trans. Green, 44).

48. Aberdeen Bestiary, folio 17r, available at https://www.abdn.ac.uk/bestiary/ms24/f17r.

49. Leclercq, *Love of Learning*, 98.

50. Leclercq, *Love of Learning*, 93.

51. Augustine, *Confessions* 8.12.

52. Dan Kimball, *How (Not) to Read the Bible: Making Sense of the Anti-women, Anti-science, Pro-violence, Pro-slavery and Other Crazy-Sounding Parts of Scripture* (Grand Rapids: Zondervan, 2020), 34.

53. Kimball, *How (Not) to Read the Bible*, 34.

54. Hugh wrote an instruction manual for novices at the monastery, *De institutione novitiorum*, that emphasizes tropology.

55. Franklin T. Harkins, "Lectio Exhortatio Debet Esse: Reading as a Way of Life at the Twelfth-Century Abbey of St. Victor," in *From Knowledge to Beatitude: St. Victor, Twelfth-Century Scholars, and Beyond; Essays in Honor of Grover A. Zinn, Jr.*, ed. E. Ann Matter and Lesley Smith (Notre Dame, IN: University of Notre Dame Press, 2016), 111.

56. Hugh of St. Victor, *De institutione novitiorum*, prol. 18, quoted in Harkins, "Lectio Exhortatio Debet Esse," 111.

57. Ryan McDermott, *Tropologies: Ethics and Invention in England, c. 1350–1600*, ReFormations: Medieval and Early Modern (Notre Dame, IN: University of Notre Dame Press, 2016), 374.

58. Hans Urs von Balthasar, *Prayer*, trans. Graham Harrison (San Francisco: Ignatius, 1986), 133.

59. Peterson, *Eat This Book*, 107.

60. Peterson, *Eat This Book*, 108.

61. Peterson, *Eat This Book*, 108.

62. One writer has even composed a Shakespeare devotional: Bob Hostetler, *The Bard and the Bible* (Franklin, TN: Worthy, 2016).

63. Mark Edmundson, *Why Read?* (New York: Bloomsbury, 2004), 56.

64. George Steiner, *Real Presences* (Chicago: University of Chicago Press, 1989), 12.

65. Steiner, *Real Presences*, 17.

66. Kathleen Norris, *The Quotidian Mysteries: Laundry, Liturgy, and "Women's Work"* (Mahwah, NJ: Paulist Press, 1998), 70.

67. Balthasar, *Prayer*, trans. Graham Harrison (San Francisco: Ignatius, 1986), 137.

68. John Henry Newman, *An Essay in Aid of a Grammar of Assent* (CreateSpace, 2016), 379.

69. Stephen Prickett, *Words and the Word: Language, Poetics and Biblical Interpretation* (Cambridge: Cambridge University Press, 1988), 217.

70. C. S. Lewis, *That Hideous Strength* (New York: Scribner, 1996), 25.

71. Lewis, *That Hideous Strength*, 19.

Chapter 7 How Can You Remember What You Read?

1. *The Lord of the Rings: The Fellowship of the Ring*, directed by Peter Jackson (Los Angeles: New Line Cinema, 2001), DVD.

2. C. S. Lewis, *The Silver Chair* (New York: HarperCollins, 2005), 26.

3. Lewis, *Silver Chair*, 27.

4. Ivan Illich, *In the Vineyard of the Text: A Commentary to Hugh's "Didascalicon"* (Chicago: University of Chicago Press, 1996), 42.

5. C. S. Lewis, *Till We Have Faces: A Myth Retold* (New York: HarperOne, 2017), 78.

6. See, e.g., Chris Armstrong, *Medieval Wisdom for Modern Christians: Finding Authentic Faith in a Forgotten Age with C. S. Lewis* (Grand Rapids: Brazos, 2016); Michael Ward, *Planet Narnia* (Oxford: Oxford University Press, 2010), and several others on Lewis's mysticism.

7. Jason Baxter, *The Medieval Mind of C. S. Lewis: How Great Books Shaped a Great Mind* (Downers Grove, IL: IVP Academic, 2022), 6.

8. Mary Carruthers, *The Craft of Thought: Meditation, Rhetoric, and the Making of Images, 400–1200* (Cambridge: Cambridge University Press, 2000), 9.

9. I first published these thoughts in part in "Who Needs Reading?," *Ekstasis*, February 2022, https://www.ekstasismagazine.com/blog/2022/who-needs-reading.

10. Carruthers, *Craft of Thought*, 65.

11. Carruthers, *Craft of Thought*, 31.

12. This discussion of memory in monasteries is found in greater detail in Carruthers, *Craft of Thought*, esp. 120–30.

13. Carruthers, *Craft of Thought*, 14.

14. Louise Cowan, *Invitation to the Classics: A Guide to Books You've Always Wanted to Read* (Grand Rapids: Baker Books, 2006), 21.

15. Marie de France, *The Lais of Marie de France*, trans. Glyn S. Burgess and Keith Busby (New York: Penguin, 1986), 126.

16. Marie de France, *Lais of Marie de France*, 41.

17. Ray Bradbury, *Fahrenheit 451* (New York: Simon & Schuster, 2012), 145.

18. Bradbury, *Fahrenheit 451*, 157.

19. Bradbury, *Fahrenheit 451*, 146.

20. Portions of this paragraph use material from Jessica Hooten Wilson, "Cormac McCarthy, Cultural Memory, and the Mythopoesis of Fire," *Church Life Journal*, October 28, 2021, https://churchlifejournal.nd.edu/articles/cormac-mccarthy-cultural-memory-and-the-mythopoesis-of-fire.

21. Flannery O'Connor, "The Fiction Writer and His Country," in *Mystery and Manners: Occasional Prose*, ed. Sally Fitzgerald and Robert Fitzgerald (New York: Farrar, Straus & Giroux, 1969), 34.

Bookmark 4 Reading like Dorothy L. Sayers

1. Dorothy L. Sayers, *The Man Born to Be King* (Eugene, OR: Wipf & Stock, 2011), 76.

2. Sayers, introduction to *The Man Born to Be King*, 10.

3. Melissa Dinsman, "Militarizing the Messiah: Britain's Wartime Rebranding in *The Man Born to Be King*," *The Space Between: Literature and Culture 1914–1945*, 11, no. 2 (2015), https://scalar.usc.edu/works/the-space-between-literature-and-culture-1914-1945/vol11_2015_dinsman.13.

4. Kenneth M. Wolfe, *The Churches and the British Broadcasting Corporation, 1922–1956: The Politics of Broadcast Religion* (London: SCM, 1984), 226.

5. Quoted in Crystal Downing, "The Transforming Imagination of Dorothy L. Sayers: Creativity for the Cause of Christ," *Wheaton Magazine* 24, no. 1 (Winter 2021), https://www.wheaton.edu/magazine/winter-2021/the-transformation-imagination-of-dorothy-l-sayers.

6. Sayers, introduction to *The Man Born to Be King*, 12.

7. Sayers, introduction to *The Man Born to Be King*, 37.

8. Sayers, introduction to *The Man Born to Be King*, 10.

9. Luther said that he would walk out in the street to hear how mothers spoke to their children and how the ordinary man spoke at the market. Eugene Peterson writes on these early vulgar translations in *Eat This Book: A Conversation in the Art of Spiritual Reading* (Grand Rapids: Eerdmans, 2009), 161.

10. Sayers, introduction to *The Man Born to Be King*, 14.

11. Sayers, introduction to *The Man Born to Be King*, 41.

12. Dorothy L. Sayers, "The Dogma Is the Drama," in *Letters to a Diminished Church: Passionate Arguments for the Relevance of Christian Doctrine* (Nashville: Thomas Nelson, 2004), 19–20.

13. Malcolm Guite, "Good Ground: A Sonnet on the Parable of the Sower," October 10, 2015, https://malcolmguite.wordpress.com/tag/parable.

14. J. Ramsey Michaels, *Passing by the Dragon* (Eugene, OR: Wipf & Stock, 2013), 9–10.

15. Dorothy L. Sayers, "The Translation of Verse," in *The Poetry of Search and the Poetry of Statement* (London: Victor Gollancz, 1963), 127.

16. Dorothy L. Sayers, *The Letters of Dorothy L. Sayers*, vol. 3, *1944–1950: A Noble Daring*, ed. Barbara Reynolds (London: Hodder & Stoughton, 1998), 77.

17. Sayers, "Translation of Verse," 152–53.

18. Dorothy L. Sayers, "On Translating *The Divina Commedia*," in *The Poetry of Search*, 91.

19. Julia Alvarez, "Bilingual Sestina," in *The Other Side: El Otro Lado* (Boston: E. P. Dutton, 1995), 3–4.

20. Owen Barfield, "Thinking and Thought," in *A Barfield Reader: Selections from the Writings of Owen Barfield*, ed. G. B. Tennyson (Middletown, CT: Wesleyan University Press, 1999), 143.

21. Scot McKnight, "The Bible Made Strange: Sarah Ruden's Four New Gospels," *Marginalia Review of Books*, December 3, 2021, https://themarginaliareview.com/the-bible-made-strange-sarah-rudens-four-new-gospels.

22. C. S. Lewis, *A Preface to Paradise Lost* (London: Oxford University Press, 1942), 64.

23. Sayers, "The Maker," in introduction to *The Man Born to Be King*, 10.

24. "Your recipe for detective fiction [is] the art of framing lies. From the beginning to the end of your book, it is your whole aim and object to lead the reader up the garden, to induce him to believe a lie." Dorothy L. Sayers, "Aristotle on Detective Fiction," quoted in Janet Hitchman, *Such a Strange Lady* (New York: Harper & Row, 1975), 65.

25. Sayers, "Aristotle on Detective Fiction," quoted in Hitchman, *Such a Strange Lady*, 65.

26. Sayers, "Aristotle on Detective Fiction," quoted by Hitchman, *Such a Strange Lady*, 68.

27. Jessica Hooten Wilson, "We're Formed by Stories. Are You Reading Good Ones?," review of *Reading Evangelicals* by Daniel Silliman, *The Gospel Coalition*, December 2, 2021, https://www.thegospelcoalition.org/reviews/reading-evangelicals.

Conclusion

1. Masha Gessen, *The Man Without a Face: The Unlikely Rise of Vladimir Putin* (New York: Riverhead, 2012).

2. Dana Gioia, "Planting a Sequoia," available at https://danagioia.com/planting-a-sequoia.

Appendix A Twofold Reading of Flannery O'Connor's "The River"

1. Flannery O'Connor, "On Her Own Work," in *Mystery and Manners: Occasional Prose*, ed. Sally Fitzgerald and Robert Fitzgerald (New York: Farrar, Straus & Giroux, 1969), 113.

2. "This is how you will know that the living God is among you" (Josh. 3:10).

3. Flannery O'Connor, "The River," in *Complete Stories* (New York: Farrar, Straus & Giroux, 1971), 174.

4. Flannery O'Connor to "A" (Betty Hester), September 6, 1955, in *The Habit of Being: The Letters of Flannery O'Connor*, ed. Sally Fitzgerald (New York: Farrar, Straus & Giroux, 1979), 100.

Appendix B Frequently Asked Questions

1. Karen Swallow Prior, *Booked: Literature in the Soul of Me* (Ossining, NY: T. S. Poetry, 2012), 19, quoting John Milton, *Areopagitica* (1644).

Appendix C Reading Lists of Great Books

1. I'm not a fan of those by their son Mike Berenstain, which tend toward didactic and preachy.